CARSON MANSION
and
INGOMAR THEATRE

William Carson.

CARSON MANSION & INGOMAR THEATRE

Cultural Adventures In California

BENJAMIN SACKS

FRESNO  1979

Copyright © 1979
Valley Publishers
All rights reserved. No part of this book may be reproduced
in any form without the written consent of the publisher.
Manufactured in the United States of America.
Valley Publishers
8 East Olive Avenue
Fresno, California 93728

Library of Congress Catalog Number 78-78378
Cloth Cover ISBN 0-913548-64-2
Soft Cover ISBN 0-913548-65-0

Contents

List of Illustrations vii
Preface ix
Foreword xv
A Theme 1
William Carson: A Sketch 11
    Entrepreneur 11
    Local Personality 18
    The Descendants 23
Carson Mansion: An Interpretation 27
    Milieu 27
    Architectural Historians 29
    Newsom Brothers, Architects 34
    Exterior Highlights 43
Carson Mansion: A Narrative 53
    Newsom Brothers, Architects 53
    Interior Highlights 55
    Construction 73
    Landscaping 80
Ingomar Theatre: A Mission 87
    Carson Block 87
    A Playhouse Wanted 89
    Construction 97
    Opening Presentation 105

CONTENTS

Ingomar the Barbarian: A Catalyst   111
    Introduction   111
    Synopsis   113
    Critiques   116

Ingomar Theatre: A Narrative   121
    Local Scene   121
    Ingomar Performances   124
    Subsequent History   128

A Trustee   137
    A Social Precedent   137
    Ingomar Club   139

Map of Humboldt County   149

Bibliography   151

Photographic References   157

Index   161
    Carson Clan   161
    Humboldt County   161
    National Roster   164

List of Illustrations

William Carson   frontispiece
Carson Mansion Front Elevation Sketch (1885)   7
Carson Mansion (1890)   8
Carson Mansion (1902)   9
Carson Mansion (Post-1914)   10
Carson Mansion (Since 1950)   10
Carson Mansion, Aerial Profile (Since 1950)   10
Side Entrance (1960)   49
Cyclopean Porch Pillars (1979)   50
Southwest Corner (1960)   50
Tower and South Gable (1960)   51
West Gable (1960)   51
Tower Profile (1960)   52
Tower Room and Balcony (1960)   52
Entry Hall (1960)   63
Stairway Hall Ceiling (1960)   64
Stained Glass Panels, Entry Hall (1979)   64
First Floor Stairway (1960)   65
Stained Glass Panel, First Floor Drawing Room (1979)   66
First Floor Drawing Room (1960)   66
First Floor Living Room (1960)   67
Dining Room (1979)   68
Stairway, Second Floor Hall (1960)   69
Second Floor Hallway (1960)   70

LIST OF ILLUSTRATIONS

Bird and Foliage Stained Glass Panel (1979)   71
Second Floor Living Room (1960)   71
Third Floor Ballroom (1979)   72
Third Floor Historic Room (1979)   72
Private Gardens (1979)   83
Private Gardens (1979)   84
Pink Lady, John Milton Carson's Home (1979)   85
Pink Lady, John Milton Carson's Home (1979)   86
Carson Block (1904)   101
Ingomar Theatre (1904)   102
Ingomar Theatre from Stage, *Cabinet Photograph, Wunderlich Bros.* (1894)   103
Ingomar Theatre (1958)   103
Enclosed Theatre Box at Upper Level (1958)   104
Ingomar Theatre Lower (Open) Boxes (1958)   104
Souvenir Program, Final Curtain Call (1958)   134
Newspaper Accounts, Final Curtain Call (1958)   135
London and Boston Programs, *Ingomar* (1851 and 1879)   136
Eureka, California (1905)   148

Preface

American civilization has been said to find its vitality in the social theory of pluralism. This thesis contends that the collective creativity of all communities in the United States is the basis for our progress. This is not to say that the national scene is devoid of inspirational leadership or exemplary accomplishments. Certainly such metropolitan centers as Washington, D.C., New York, Chicago, and Los Angeles do provide the most pregnant experiences in the way of cultural events. But the audiences are not just city folk, claiming as well visitors from small towns and the countryside. If this approach offers some sort of bridge between two sources of enrichment, the bond is drawn tighter by the modern means of mass communications, namely radio and television. Still the value of self-participation at the grass roots level is not to be discounted, for not only does it yield a better appreciation of refinement but also an opportunity to reflect the views of the people.

Even more dependent upon themselves for cultural nourishment were communities in the decades considered in this study. The town of Eureka was no exception to these generalizations, borrowing from the national scene and contributing to the national heritage. This is the story unfolded in the following chapters and it is hoped that the result may be to place local history and the national background in the proper perspective.

It should be pointed out that a purposeful methodology has been employed. The approach in the case of both the Carson Mansion and Ingomar Theatre has been from the general to the particular. If some of the material thus included might seem extraneous to the local story (although in itself culturally enriching), the answer is that the narrower subject can only be confirmed in its significance by establishing a continuity with the broader perspective. The Carson Mansion should be related to an architecture that had swept the country and of which it became a prime and celebrated example. Architectural historians never fail to mention it in their accounts of the Gothic Revival, offering interpretations as to its place among the varied styles. The Ingomar Theatre had its genesis in a play which received wide acclaim in the second half of the nineteenth century, testified to by the frequent productions in leading cities and by the distinguished roster of those enacting the major roles. That the play, both in the flesh and in commemorative nomenclature, should find a warm reception in outlying areas spoke volumes for the growing unity of the nation. In short, the experiences detailed in Eureka, leading metropolis of Humboldt County, afford a graphic illustration that local history in a broader setting emerges with dignity at an intellectual level.

To provide a coherent thread for this ambitious blueprint, some observations would seem in order. The first two chapters speak for themselves, setting forth the continuing vitality of the subject matter to be treated and the relevant biographical facts about the central figure in the story responsible for the edifice and the theater. The third and fourth chapters relate to the Carson Mansion. Where the former places the emphasis upon the national context, the latter focuses the spotlight upon the local setting. It is hoped that the total accomplishment will be to explore in depth for the reader the acculturation process through the medium of architecture. The fifth through the seventh chapters relate to what may be called the Ingomar syndrome. The fifth chapter reverses the sequence of acculturation, dealing with the provision of a theater to enrich the life of a frontier community. The sixth chapter turns to the broader picture of the national matrix, examining the specific dramatic play upon which the hopes of the local cultural leaders were pinned for nurturing human sensitivity. The seventh chapter describes how a somewhat isolated settlement reacted to the purposeful efforts to link itself with the mainstream of a country's search for a civilization. The hope is that the sum result will offer a substantive insight for the reader of the acculturation process through the medium of the theater. The eighth and final chapter may be described as a potpourri projecting the fortunes of the two experiments as revivifying factors in a current nourishment of the value of this heritage.

The relative scarcity of information devoted to the region of northern California beyond the San Francisco Bay region in scholarly books has been markedly evident in the search for pertinent literature. The broadly-based studies generally must be faulted in their tendency to hurry on from the Golden Gate city to Oregon and Washington in their accounts of the Pacific slope. Such is the fact, for example, in Professor Earl Pomeroy's admirable book, *The Pacific Slope: A History* (1965), in which, indeed, the map of the American West does not even contain the location of Eureka. Nor does his earlier and equally perceptive book, *In Search of the Golden West: The Tourist in Western America* (1957) suggest any local attractions "as indexes to general social development" in Humboldt County. Perhaps the omissions are a reflection of the lack of solid monographs about the various aspects of life in the redwood country. Certainly the many untapped sources in the form of unpublished manuscripts and primary sources discovered in the libraries of the area offer opportunities for topical monographs. Furthermore, it is hoped that this study might spur an interest among local inhabitants to come forward with additional source material and for old-timers to welcome the occasion to share their rich experiences. The net result could well be a series of more comprehensive histories that would assure northern California of its deserved role in the story of the Pacific slope.

In this connection, a confession by the author would seem in order. During his academic career the field of preoccupation had been nineteenth and twentieth century British history. It was with some trepidation that this venture into the American West was undertaken. Moreover, the cultural aspects of a provincial region were to be the center of attraction whereas the lifelong arena of research had been in political, social, and imperial crises at a national level of interest. The challenge was to acquire a new historical background and to gather an understanding of the vocabulary in the branches of architecture and the drama. The knowledge that others had done so provided me with some degree of reassurance for this venture. In particular, I would refer to a preface in a study by Professor Harold Melvin Hyman, *Soldiers and Spruce: Origins of the Loyal Legion of Loggers and Lumbermen* (1966), examined as possible literature bearing upon the topic at hand. While his lapse for the moment was not quite as precipitous as mine, simply transferring from one period (Civil War and Reconstruction) to another (World War I) of American history, he expressed a certain hesitation in the decision to enter virgin territory. What bolstered his courage and supplied me with a possible rationale was a reference to advice proffered by Professor Samuel Eliot Morison to students of history in his address as president of the American Historical Association on December 29, 1950, at Chicago (reprinted in the *American Historical Review*, January 1951, p. 271):

"... Everyone should, I believe, study something general or national in scope and something special or local; should do research on a remote period or on a contemporary period, and work on more than one type of history. The national field teaches you what to look for in local history; whilst intensive cultivation of grass-roots ... teaches you things that you cannot see in the broad national view. Local history as a sideline also serves to integrate a historian with his community, to make him a valued and respected member of it, instead of 'just another professor.'"

Some practices in spelling and footnote citations require clarification. If the Eurekans used the spelling "theatre" for their playhouse, the alternate spelling "theater" has been adopted in speaking of a playhouse in generality. In this connection, after the initial introduction of the full title of the play, *Ingomar the Barbarian*, it will be usually shortened to *Ingomar*. A similar move for economy of space has been made with regard to the two major local newspapers which constitute the heart of the primary sources. So instead of the *Daily Humboldt Times* and the *Daily Humboldt Standard*, it will be the *Times* and the *Standard* until the two merged in 1968 as the *Times-Standard*. Only if the newspaper is a weekly edition of either one or the other will the full nomenclature be given. It might further be said that, apart from the editorials and foreign extracts, the weekly issues repeat the local news items in the dailies. But care should be taken, if only the weekly issue is available, to establish accurately the chronology of individual local items borrowed from the dailies. In the case of the *Susie Baker Fountain Papers*, the practice will be to shorten the identification to the *Fountain Papers*. References to the college at Arcata are given the nomenclature of the particular period being discussed—Humboldt State College or Humboldt State University.

The decision to integrate the footnote citations in the body of the text is prompted by the particular nature of the material. To have adhered to the traditional scholarly technique would have made difficult any smooth continuity in the story. Indeed, the alternative would have had to be the omnibus footnote. In the case of books cited, their authors are coupled with the dates of publications and perhaps the specific paginations where indexes are lacking. The full identification, of course, may be found in the bibliography. The significant factor in this methodology is the achievement of some degree of flexibility in dealing with cultural history.

Acknowledgements are due many people for the realization of this study. Erich F. Schimps, associate librarian and curator of the special collections room at Humboldt State University, helped in numerous ways. He facilitated the loan of local newspapers and books and called attention to the availability of pertinent manuscripts. He made arrangements for valuable contacts with knowledgeable persons in Humboldt County. He reviewed the manuscript and his knowledge of landscaping and local history saved me from many an error. Lawrence Dever, reference librarian at the Eureka-Humboldt Public Library, aided in the loan of material and answered inquiries patiently. The services of Wilber Leeds, Certified

PREFACE

Genealogical Record Searcher, San Francisco, and of Peter E. Palmquist, a professional photographer in the Eureka-Arcata area, are both gratefully acknowledged. Mrs. Georgina Peyton, head of the Mandeville department of special collections at the University of California, San Diego, provided expertise in running down much-needed items. Frequent recourse was had to Donald McKie and Larry Cruse in the government documents section at the University of California, San Diego. In the middle of all this hectic searching were Mrs. Frances Ness and Mrs. Elaine Banks, interlibrary loan staff members at the University of California, San Diego. Their cooperation went beyond the line of duty for over a year; from their desks flowed a steady stream of requests for books, journals, and newspapers (in microfilm). To those institutions which were accommodating in interlibrary loans a vote of thanks is owed—the University of California at both Los Angeles and Berkeley (Bancroft Library) and Humboldt State University.

The role of an armchair historian was supplemented by trips to several libraries. The California Room at the San Diego Public Library had a number of pertinent items. The Special Collections Room at the University of California at Los Angeles provided related literature. In the San Francisco Bay area there were visits to the Bancroft Library and other depositories on the Berkeley campus. In the Golden City itself the San Francisco Public Library and the California Historical Society Library were explored. The State Library at Sacramento possessed a considerable amount of material, especially in the way of newspapers. The culminating destination was Eureka-Arcata, where extended stays assured the procurement of the rest of the documentary sources stored at Humboldt State University. Interviews with county residents versed in the historical heritage of the Humboldt region filled in many gaps. Their number prevents any singling out but their aid is not forgotten. The current occupant of what used to be the Carson Block housing the Ingomar Theatre took time out to show me around and to explain features of the dismantled playhouse. Most gratifying was the opportunity afforded by members of the Ingomar Club to tour the interior of Carson Mansion and to see things for myself firsthand. But the responsibility for the contents—data, arrangement, interpretation—is, of course, my own.

Foreword

The Carson Mansion is probably the most familiar landmark in Northwestern California to many thousands of Americans. Hundreds of amateur and professional photographers have captured its beauty on film, and so many pictures of the mansion have been reproduced in so many magazines and other publications that it is said to be the "most photographed house in America." Many famous artists have depicted its beauty in paintings which hang in many homes in America. The Carson Mansion has long been recognized by architects as undoubtedly the most perfect example of the so-called "Victorian" style of architecture remaining in the United States today.

The year that the mansion was built by William Carson, 1885, was a most significant year. It was a year of depression when the market for redwood lumber had reached a saturation point and the price of redwood fell. Hundreds of men were dismissed by the lumber companies and walked the streets of Eureka begging for food. A Welfare Committee was appointed in Eureka to provide food and shelter for those most in need. William Carson was a member of this committee. Perhaps he decided to build his stately mansion in 1885 to provide much needed work for his unemployed workers. Certainly, as many as one hundred workmen were employed at one time in various phases of the construction.

Eighteen-eighty-five was a notable year in other ways, too. On July 4, the Humboldt County Board of Supervisors invited the Masonic Lodge (Humboldt Lodge No. 79, F. and A.M.) to lay the cornerstone for the new county courthouse on the city block known as the "Plaza," between I and J, and Fourth and Fifth Streets. After appropriate ceremonies, James Simpson began the construction of a new and imposing courthouse which added greatly to the prestige of Eureka.

In 1885, John Vance introduced incandescent lighting to the city when he decided to use electricity to light his hotel and mill. Many businessmen along Second Street also lighted their stores with the electricity from the "electric machine" in Vance's Mill.

On February 6, 1885, Eureka city councilman David Kendall was killed by a stray bullet fired by rival tongs in Eureka's Chinatown, located between E and F, and Fourth and Fifth Streets. The resulting outcry brought about the expulsion of the Chinese from the city.

That year also saw the entry into Eureka of the Eel River and Eureka Railroad, a line that eventually became a link in the rail service to San Francisco. The City of Eureka declared a holiday on July 17, 1885, and a sixteen-car excursion train carried spectators over the new line.

During the year two events of literary importance occurred in Eureka: a significant history of the Indian troubles in Humboldt County, *Indian Wars of the Northwest*, by A. J. Bledsoe, was published; and Ashley Bancroft arrived in the city to do research on the area for the Hubert Howe Bancroft publication on California.

The famed Carson Mansion was built, therefore, in a most auspicious year in the history of Eureka.

In March of 1950, the Carson Mansion was sold to a business and professional men's group which assured the landmark's preservation. This group later became known as the Ingomar Club.

> Hyman Palais
> Professor, Humboldt State University
> History Department

CHAPTER ONE

A THEME

URING A TOUR OF THE American Far West a few years ago, an overnight stay was spent in Eureka, California. As the motor bus entered the downtown district the escort pointed out the lofty tower and spire of a residence rising conspicuously above the city. It was the Carson Mansion, renowned as a lovely example of Gothic Revival architecture such as mushroomed in towns and countryside along the Pacific coast during the second half of the nineteenth century. Leisure time was available for a visit to the site. While the interior is not open to the public, the steady stream of sightseers snapping pictures of the exterior and the landscaped grounds testified to its fame.

Curiosity propelled me to the local public library where a staff member, in response to my inquiry for literature on the subject, drew from the stacks a slender book of twenty-three pages. The author was Lawrence "Scoop" Beal, one-time editor of a local newspaper. The date of publication was 1973. The title was *William Carson's Redwood Castle*. The contents included a brief biography, a description of some of the rooms, staircases, and hallways, and a copy of Carson's will as published in a local newspaper. The fact was stressed that the residence commanded distinction as the most photographed home in the world as well as having been shot from every angle—from fire truck, airplane, helicopter, dirigible—and drawn in crayon, pencil, and ink.

In support of this proud claim Beal (as well as other writers encountered) cites an imposing list of popular journals which display profiles of the Carson Mansion. Curiosity led me to run down this generalization into specific issues which yielded an interesting assortment of data. *Overland Monthly* (January 1909) carries an industrial and historical report of Humboldt County along with its photograph. An account in the *National Geographic Magazine* (February 1909) contains a picture of the "castlelike home" as a "showcase of woodworkers' skill." *Coronet* (March 1948) features it as a symbol of the wealth that the forest brought to northern California. The oval frame scene in the *Saturday Evening Post* (November 8, 1958, p. 120) is actually an advertisement of a lumber company extolling the acoustical and insulating qualities of the redwood tree. The full page photograph in *Life* (March 5, 1956, p. 88) relates to a series entitled "America's Arts and Skills." The Carson Mansion is depicted as belonging to an age of gilded opulence, disrobing "Victorian Grandeur at its gaudiest." *House Beautiful* (February 1965, p. 99) offers similarly a full page photograph along with an article, "The Impatient Evolution of the American House." *Sunset Magazine* (October 1970, central edition) presents a view through a window of the "other Carson House across M Street," built by the father for his eldest son, John Milton, in 1889 as a wedding gift.

Indeed, the ubiquity of the Carson Mansion photograph proved endless. The Notifier Corporation of Lincoln, Nebraska published a handbill advertisement (undated but after 1950) singling out the Carson Mansion as protected from fire by its alarm system. Included are five photos—profile, front doors, front stairway, main living room, second story hallway. *Motorland* (July-August 1961) acquainted the touring public with its beauty by devoting the cover page to the profile of the Carson Mansion. The *Times Magazine* (July 1, 1957, p. 45) displayed a profile with the caption "Time for meekness when you try to better it," words borrowed from James M. (Peter Pan) Barrie. It is a review of a book written by John Maass, a German immigrant who describes himself as "an amateur fancier of architecture," entitled *The Gingerbread Age*, to be discussed in a succeeding chapter. Both the *San Francisco Chronicle* (July 31, 1960) and the *Los Angeles Times* (January 18, 1976) in their Sunday magazine sections of "Bonanza" and "Home" respectively have enlarged photographs. The news story in the latter examines the youthful writers' colony in nearby Ferndale seeking to revitalize a "gone-to-pasture dairy community." Equally proud of the state's heritage in Eureka was the *California Highway Patrolman*, including a photograph of the Carson Mansion along with an article entitled "A Backwards Glance at Eureka" in its issue of March 1950.

In the local area of Humboldt County itself the community is reminded frequently of its treasure. The Eurekan newspapers carry pictures of the profile and the interior on occasions relevant to the subject. The telephone directory of Humboldt County, October 1959, featured the residence on its cover page. The Ingomar Club (which now owns the property) puts out a wine list displaying the profile and containing a summarized account of the residence and an explanation of the Ingomar nomenclature. A recent brochure of the Eureka chamber of commerce presents a pencilled sketch of the front facade and boasts of it as the "most photographed house in America, the Queen of Victorian architecture." The Humboldt Federal Savings and Loan Association distributed a map of the region with a picture of the Carson Mansion on the outside. Not to be outdone, a food market located on Fifth and L Streets has affixed on an interior wall two blown-up photographs, one of the profile and the other of the dining room, with a proud poster proclaiming them "The World Famous Carson Mansion." Finally, not to overdo the local manifestations, the Eureka Redwood Company in a brochure of 1954 proudly proclaimed the quality of its products with the picture of the Carson Mansion.

Equally rewarding in terms of yield was the follow-up of Beal's generalization that Hollywood had been aware of the Carson Mansion's potential as a prop for western films. Perhaps the most notable movie is *Ruggles of Red Gap*, of which there were two silent and one sound productions (1923, 1928, 1935). It is the silent film of 1923 by Paramount which was done on location, starring Charles Ogle, Edward Horton, and Louise Dresser among others, and directed by James Cruze. A company of thirty-five came to Eureka in June for ten days. To quote the *Times* (July 3, 1923), "the closing scenes were enacted at the beautiful Carson House.... The lawn... already beautiful with shrubbery and flowers was made more picturesque by the addition of redwoods, which were planted bodily about the grounds...." Considering the formidable size of redwoods, one must be amazed at the boldness of the Hollywood script to achieve such a transplant. Perhaps the redwoods now near the private garden are those. Subsequently, October 22-24, 1923, when *Ruggles of Red Gap* was shown in a local movie house, the advertisement carried prominently the words "Made in Eureka."

Even more persistent were the promoters of *The Valley of the Giants*, for all three productions (1919, 1927, 1938) were shot in Humboldt County. Again it was the silent film, released by Paramount in 1919 and starring Wallace Reid, which included scenes taken at the Carson Mansion. Hundreds of local people were used and the rest of the population watched the dangerous episodes of crumbling bridges and railroad wrecks. A local movie house in Eureka was given the rare privilege of a first showing in September 1919. The *Standard*, in its issues of September 4 and 5, 1919, noted that "the old Carson home at the foot of Second Street and that of Sumner Carson (the second son, whose home was at Seventh and J Streets) were used for many of the inside scenes."

For the collector of bizarre and exotic items there are still other memorabilia to be encountered. Available in Eureka in gift shops, drugstores, restaurants, and bookstores are postcards of varying sizes featuring the residence. Recently there appeared on the market a jigsaw puzzle displaying on the outside of the packaged box a gorgeous close-up picture with all the gingerbread effects clearly delineated. The courageous player who endeavors to put the puzzle together should emerge an expert on the exterior of the Carson Mansion. It is to be hoped that future reproductions will alter the date of construction in its descriptive summary from the erroneous 1866 to 1884-1885. Finally, although the exposures seem inexhaustible, there is the use of the Carson Mansion as background in nationally syndicated comic strips. Leslie Turner in his drawings for the *Captain Easy* episodes shows the profile in the local newspaper (*Times,* April 9-16, 1963). In the seventies, Al Vemeer, who resides in Humboldt County, likewise employed it for his comic strip, *Priscilla's Pop.*

Perhaps the most unusual testimony may be found in the March 12, 1945 issue of the *Standard.* The reference is to a short story in the *Saturday Evening Post* (January 27, 1945, p. 16 et seq.) by Glenn Allan entitled "A House for My Father." It is the son who recounts the experience of his parents upon arriving in a new town for the father to work as a log scaler in a lumber mill. The father prefers a residence near the factory (even though the district is run down) so that he might enjoy the sound of the ripsaw buzzing forth from the mill. The resigned realtor shows them a grand mansion of thirty rooms known as Crayton Towers, now vacated because of the dismal surroundings. The son describes the exterior as having turreted towers, gabled roofs, bay windows filled with stained glass, bracketed cornices, lacework, and lighting rods with brass balls at their summits. Inside there are oiled panels on the walls, a grand parlor, a fireplace with a mantel of yellow marble quaintly carved, a massive ballroom, and a billiard room. The illustrator assigned by the *Post* did his sketch without any communications from the author as to whether he had any particular model in mind. The scene now shifts to Guy A. Moore of Arcata (ten miles north of Eureka) who read the article and saw the sketch of Crayton Towers in the magazine. The resemblance to the Carson Mansion seemed remarkable, notwithstanding high chimneys and the small balcony *above* the tower. Moore sent a letter to the associate editor and included a picture of the Carson Mansion. The latter forwarded the letter and the picture to the illustrator who affirmed a connection:

> "The author had that house in mind. Of course I had to follow his description and not knowing that he had that house in mind I

went through the New York library research department and that was the only 'gingerbread' type of house that I could find, and it seemed to fill the bill.

Mr. Allan wondered how I happened to pick the same house. As a matter of fact, I think it's the only one of its kind, so I didn't go any further. But I did have to sort of wreck the house in my picture (by putting in the high chimneys and the balcony *aloft* the tower)."

The *Standard* headed its account with pictures of the Carson Mansion and Crayton Towers side by side.

To run the full gamut of its widespread popularity and renown, the historians of American architecture have made the Carson Mansion a part of the national heritage. Maass in his books on Victorian homes in the United States includes the original front elevation sketch by the architects as well as black-and-white and color photographs. Dr. David Gebhard, professor of architectural history and director of the Art Museum, University of California, Santa Barbara, in works written in collaboration with other students of California architecture, rates "the well-known Carson House . . . [as] a structure which certainly represents the high point of the early Queen Anne in the United States." Dr. Harold Kirker, professor of history at the same institution, in discussing architectural style and tradition in the nineteenth century, pays tribute to the Carson Mansion as one of the finest surviving examples of Victorian residences in America. He includes also the front elevation sketch and a photograph of the exterior. Edward Geoffrey Bangs, a member of the Northern California Chapter of the American Institute of Architects, in his book sponsored by the California Historical Society, avers that "every collection of early California architecture should certainly include this masterpiece of Victorian art." Marshall B. Davidson, editor of a prestigious book on notable American houses (as well as others), praises the Carson Mansion and includes the familiar front elevation sketch. And in a very recent two-volume elegant set under his editorship and authored by G. E. Kidder Smith, architectural writer and photographer, the profile of the Carson Mansion is presented as "what is probably the finest late Victorian exterior in the country, a culmination of profligate fancies haughtily but gloriously dispensed."

Whether or not any claim could be made of equal fame abroad, only one article was encountered in foreign periodicals. Georg Gerster deals with "Das Carson-Haus in Eureka" in the *Bauwelt* (April 21, 1969), an architectural journal published in Berlin. The short account opens in a somewhat macabre spirit, referring to the foggy weather in Eureka as the worst in the United States. So well known was this fact of frequency and density of Eureka fog that during World War II an Air Force-Naval-

Civil Landing Aids experiment station was set up at the local field for fog dispersal operations as an alternative to the expense of preparing artificially activated conditions to simulate zero visibility. Indeed, on two of the three occasions I flew into the Eureka-Arcata airport (located at McKinleyville a few miles to the north) the airline representative at San Francisco alerted passengers that it might not be possible to make a landing. Fortunately, each time the mist cleared or opened briefly to permit a descent. At any rate, apparently the information supplied to Gerster by the Eureka chamber of commerce suggested that the latter found the notoriety given the foggy climate embarrassing in promoting the growth of the city. But instead of submitting an impressive statistical record, the article explained to German readers that the Eureka chamber of commerce would prefer to focus attention upon a superlative, namely the Carson Mansion. To that end a brief description was given of the residence built in 1885 by a lumber and shipping magnate as "living quarters for his family, a unique, opulent witness to Victorian buildings, . . . the most marvelled about and photographed in America." For the rest, the article lists some of the elegant materials used, the role of William Carson in overseeing its construction and leaving his imprint upon the structure, and the effectiveness of the private club now in possession of the property in preserving the historical edifice. Several photographs are included—the hallway on the second floor, the bizarre pillars supporting the front porch, the fabulous gingerbread adorning the outer facade, and a sort of aerial view looking down upon the exterior profile.

To turn back to Beal's book, one sentence in the narrative particularly arrested my attention. The statement is made that William Carson had constructed a modern playhouse which he named the Ingomar Theatre "after his favorite stage play, *Ingomar the Barbarian*." My imagination was further stirred by the fact that the Carson Mansion is now the home of a social organization known as the Ingomar Club and so marked by signposts erected on the front lawn. Through my mind coursed the thought that perhaps there was some deeper cultural affinity worthy of study embracing the Carson Mansion and the Ingomar nomenclature. It is hoped that this venture in Western Americana offers some insight into the acculturation process during the frontier decades of Pacific coast history.

1885 architect's drawing of front elevation of Carson Mansion by Newsom Brothers.

1890 scene as shown in *Fine California Views* by Peter Palmquist.

1902 scene from *Humboldt County Souvenir* and *Historic American Buildings Survey*, 1960.

Post-1914 scene with shrubbery.

Aerial profile of Ingomar Club.

Since 1950—Ingomar Club, front view.

CHAPTER TWO

William Carson: A Sketch

Entrepreneur

HE SALIENT FACTS in the life of William Carson should provide a substantive background. The material has emerged as a hard core of data repeated constantly in the literature. It is hoped that some new details and corrections have been contributed here. The most fruitful sources in the bibliography are as follows: (1) Palais and Roberts, "The History of the Lumber Industry in Humboldt County," *Pacific Historical Review*, February 1950; (2) Gordon, "Humboldt Lumber Mills," *Wood and Iron*, August 1904; a reprint is available in the *Standard*, August 4, 1904; (3) Melendy, *One Hundred Years of the Redwood Industry, 1850-1950* (1952); (4) Melendy, "Two Men and a Mill: John Dolbeer, William Carson and the Redwood Lumber Industry in California," *California Historical Society Quarterly*, (1959); (5) *Standard*, December 31, 1883 and December 31, 1891 (interviews with William Carson); (6) *Fountain Papers, passim*; (7) *Dolbeer and Carson Lumber Company, Business Papers, passim*; (8) Edgar Cherry and Company, *Redwood and Lumbering in California Forests* (1884).

William Carson was born on July 15, 1825 in Charlotte County not far from Elmsville, in the eastern Canadian province of New Brunswick. He had no middle name and the confusion came about in the following manner. Dr. Joseph Armstrong Baird, Jr., architectural historian and formerly with the California Historical Society, in his data book report of the Carson Mansion for the Historic American Buildings Survey (1964) offers McKendrie as the middle name. The only book which repeats this is

Maass's *The Victorian Home in America* (1972, p. 165), and the evidence indicates he picked it up from Baird. But I did not find any other materials—news items, obituaries, books—carrying McKendrie or any other middle name. Subsequently I wrote to Baird in San Francisco where he is an art consultant and he cited as his source a scrapbook in the holdings of the library of the California Historical Society. The reply of the latter body included a copy of a news item quoting an excerpt from the diary of William "McKendrie" Carson of his arrival in San Francisco in February 1849, now in the possession of his granddaughter. The details made it quickly evident that a case of mistaken identity was involved. The particular pioneer arrived a year before our personage, in a different ship (*Jane Parker*), came from Maryland, engaged in farming near Stockton, and was a Methodist. A letter from the granddaughter (Mrs. Howard M. Gunton, Oakland) confirmed these facts. While an inquiry was addressed to pertinent authorities in New Brunswick, Canada, the archives were lacking for the year of his birth to corroborate the above facts.

At an early age William Carson helped his father (an immigrant from Northern Ireland) stockpile lumber for freighters. In 1849, along with other youths, he joined the gold rush to California, reaching the Pacific coast via Cape Horn on the *Brazilian* after a voyage of seven months. Arriving in San Francisco in April 1850, his first job was rolling out by hand gold bars from which fifty-dollar slugs were then made. His next move was to Sonoma where he purchased a pack of horses from Mexicans and proceeded to the gold fields along the Trinity River. However, pickings were meager and in the winter of 1850-51 the youthful band visited neighboring Humboldt County where game was plentiful. For a while, presumably using his pack of horses, he hauled logs from the Freshwater Slough to the water's edge from whence they were rafted to the Pioneer Mill. Later, Carson claimed that he had felled the first tree ever in the area for commercial purposes, a spruce measuring 140 feet to the first limb. The spring of 1851 found him back again in the Trinity gold fields. The new tactic was to change the course of the river for three-quarters of a mile with logs and earth in the belief that gold might be taken from the original bed if laid bare for the miner's pick. David E. Gordon, a local veteran newspaperman, asserts in his account to have heard from the lips of Carson a reference to his early California days that "I lived in Trinity County once for less than a year, took a hand in the Arkansaw Dam venture which the flood wiped out." For a corroboratory statement actually listing William Carson as one of the participants see Carr *Pioneer Days in California* (1891, p. 141ff).

Carson found his real gold in the forests concentrated along the coast of northern California with its heart in Humboldt County. The unique presence of the redwood only in this region was held to be due to the high degree of moisture generated by the fog belt along the local coast where clear days numbered about forty annually. Because of the tremendous size and weight of the redwood it could not be handled and sawed with the primitive facilities available to the pioneer lumbermen. So the manufacture of lumber at first had been confined to pine, spruce, and Douglas fir, which were easier to fell, to log, and to mill. But Carson was not to be overawed and challenged the giant redwood, which averaged about eight feet or more in diameter and upwards of two hundred feet in height. In the spring of 1852, according to Professor Hyman Palais, longtime member of the department of history at Humboldt State University, Carson purchased a team of oxen in Sacramento and went to work as a logging contractor for Ryan and Duff. His source was a pamphlet he read in the business papers of the Dolbeer and Carson Lumber Company, reprinted in the *West Coast Lumbermen* (June 1939) entitled "Since 1863." By 1854 Carson was operating the Muley Mill (named after the upright type of saw first used), toiling as a sawyer, foreman, and salesman. Indeed, as he recalled those early days, he labored as sawyer for the day shift and every other night as well. Soon he had leased a mill at the foot of I Street in Eureka, consolidating logging and milling under one management. Within a year, as he told reporters in interviews, he shipped the initial cargo of redwoods milled in Humboldt County. In July 1855, he sold some 130,000 board feet at the price of $25 per 1,000 board feet for dispatch to San Francisco on the brigs *Quoddy Belle* and *Tigris*.

Environmentalists today take a critical view of the large-scale logging of the majestic redwoods. As a matter of fact, the book published by Edgar Cherry and Company in 1884 does discuss the problem of timber culture and the responsibility of reproduction for the aesthetic and practical needs of future generations. However, in the nineteenth century, the use of timber as a building material made possible the settlement of communities on the Pacific coast and inland. Carson never failed to note the superior qualities of the redwood which made human habitation something more than camping out. It had a very pleasing color which varied from light cherry to dark mahogany, and took a fine polish. It did not rot or decay and was impervious to the onslaught of insects. Nor would it swell or warp if properly treated. Furthermore, it had proven to possess non-combustible qualities by reason of the absence of pitch and resinous matter. If fires were frequent at mills, it was because millmen were careless about cleaning sawdust off the beams, thus exposing the dry sawdust to ignition by flying sparks. As for the uses to which the redwood could be employed better than other woods, the list was endless. Industrially, the applications included pickets and posts for fencing, railroad ties, decks and hulls for ships, and the construction of bridges. For the exterior of buildings the durability of the redwood made excellent shingles and shakes for roofing, sidings, and structural foundations. For the interior of offices and homes, its fine polish and colors provided beautiful floors, stairways, paneling, moldings, grooved ceilings, doors, and window frames. For furniture the list embraced bureaus, bedsteads, sideboards, and picture frames.

For the next decade Carson would seem to have been involved in various lumber activities, leasing mills and negotiating for timberlands. But success was by no means a continuous process. There were occasional fires at individual mills. The schooners had their problems getting in and out of the bay, while at sea they faced the terrors of storms and gales. What enabled Carson to forge ahead was his partnership with John Dolbeer, a native of New Hampshire, consummated and signed on April 17, 1863. Dolbeer had an inventive mind and revolutionized the method of snaking the huge redwoods out of ravines and hillsides. Known as the steam donkey (and often referred to as the steam-bull team or the donkey engine), this mechanism hauled the felled logs to the open trail. From there an oxen team pulled the spoils of the axe along a skid road (greased transverse logs) to landings at tidewater, to be rafted to the mill or loaded on railway open flats. Dolbeer patented his single cylinder side-spool contrivance and other lumber companies were quick to adopt it.

Despite a fire in 1878 which destroyed the Bay Mill with a loss estimated at $50,000, the Dolbeer and Carson Lumber Company prospered. The two partners divided the responsibilities, the former handling marketing and financial matters in San Francisco and the latter settling in Eureka to manage the production end. For an exceptionally detailed description of the technical processes, from the logging of the timber to the product turned out by the mill, see Edgar Cherry and Company, *Redwood and Lumbering in California Forests* (1884).

Carson provided local newspaper reporters with an inventory of the company's holdings. The firm owned 20,000 acres of the finest redwoods in the world. They had bought up timberland in the Elk River area and Lindsey Creek. Their Bay Mill along the foot of the Eureka wharf with plenty of front and boom privileges for floating logs had a capacity of 70,000 feet daily. Apparently it had been acquired by Dolbeer, and after the fire in 1878, had been promptly rebuilt and moved near the foot of L Street. Bay Mill had kept pace with the latest equipment, notably the circular saw, the bandsaw, and the turning lathe. An interesting story in the Palais article (co-authored with Earl Roberts, a local high school teacher) concerned the question of dovetailing the operations at Bay Mill and at Salmon Creek (some thirty miles south of Eureka). Against the advice of Dolbeer, Carson bought a mill there in 1878 for summer operation when transportation was practical. His plan was to use the Bay Mill in the winter and then transfer his crew to Salmon Creek in the summer. When the company's cash flow got tight, Carson conceived the idea to form the Milford Land Company and to sell stock (which was later bought back). As an item of interest, the second year's report of the chamber of commerce in 1884 listed the annual capacity of Bay Mill at 15,000,000 feet and the Salmon Creek mill at 12,000,000 feet against an actual production of 15,000,000 feet for the two together in 1884. But after logging methods and transportation facilities were improved, the need for the Salmon Creek mill ended and the Milford Land Company was dissolved.

In addition, according to Carson's inventory, by the 1890s there were three shingle mills, one at Bay Mill, a second at Brainard's Point near Jacoby Creek (northeast of Eureka), and a third at Willow Creek (near Salmon Creek), producing a total of 130,000 shingles daily. Later a fourth would seem to have been acquired, known as the Milford Mill at Salmon Creek. For a supplementary or alternative means of transportation the firm had promoted several railroad lines. It held a half interest in the Bucksport and Elk River Railroad, a narrow gauge line of some twelve miles extending from Bucksport and Field's Landing to an Elk River terminus at Falk. Besides providing an access to redwood resources, the road accommodated the trade of Elk River Valley. Even more fully owned by Carson and Dolbeer was the Eel River and Eureka Railroad, a standard gauge line planned for a score or more miles extending from Eureka to Hydesville and Alton in the south. Besides providing an access to timber resources, the road passed through a strip of rich farming land which raised grain, hay, and potatoes. For some of the atmosphere connected with its construction the reader is referred to the brief account in Kneiss's *Redwood Railways* (1956). The firm also gave support to the construction of a railroad northward from Eureka to Arcata and on to Samoa and Fieldbrook known as the Humboldt Northern Railroad, with the hope of tapping timber resources and injecting new life into the area.

The major terminus for the lumber was San Francisco where the booming Bay region settlements called for the construction of homes, buildings, bridges, and railroad lines. As for foreign ports, Carson listed the destinations for his firm's lumber as far south as Guaymas, San Diego, Los Angeles, and San Pedro and as far west as the Sandwich Islands, Sydney, and the Orient. If it seems far-fetched that the Sandwich Islands were included in the itineraries, the answer is that the Hawaiian Islands were often so referred to in the nineteenth century. On special occasions cargoes were sent to the British Isles although steady trade with Europe awaited the completion of a canal across the isthmus of Central America.

To safeguard the trade from ruthless and ruinous competition among the several rival mills, Carson spearheaded the organization of the Humboldt Lumber Manufacturers' Association and served actively as president and a member of the board of directors. It handled the negotiations for the shipments of lumber abroad, presumably allotting quotas to affiliates and assuring fairness to the producers as well as quality to the consumers. The association also operated the tugs *Relief* and *Ranger* over the Humboldt sand bar. For an excellent book on the lumber industry, see Thomas R. Cox, *Mills and Markets: A History of the Pacific Coast Lumber Industry to 1900* (1974).

Carson listed some of the vessels in which Dolbeer and he had shares, usually in the percentage of two-sixteenths or two-thirty-seconds. Apart from whatever dividends might be derived from their general operations, the guarantee of vessels being available for their lumber trade was assured. The steamer schooners *Oneatta* and *Farallon* plied the local waters. The barkentine *William Carson* was a three-mast vessel having the foremast square-rigged and the two aftermasts fore-and-aft rigged. It had a tragic story, for scarcely one year had elapsed since its launching when in 1899 a collision near the Hawaiian Islands sent it to the bottom of the ocean. More enduring was the story of the schooner *Lottie Carson*, named after his daughter Carlotta. It was sold in 1912 and the new owner changed its name to the *Leonora*. In 1936 the schooner was laid up in Newport Harbor and then refitted in 1941 after which it is reputed to have appeared in several films.

The majority of their shares, however, were in schooners, by this time usually possessing three masts and fore-and-aft rigged sails, although some such vessels came to have four and more masts. One is reminded of what they looked like by the so-called "tall ships" made memorable during the American Bicentennial in the summer of 1976. Initially these vessels included the *Lottie Carson, Halcyon, Edward Parke, Volant, Bertha Dolbeer, Sequoia,* and *Mabel Gray,* totalling a carrying capacity of three million feet of lumber. Later additions were *S. T. Alexander, Azalea, Eclipse, Glencoe, Iaqua, Hesperian, Maweema, Metha Nelson,* and *Wawona*. For sources containing the percentages of shares, technical details, and ownership transfers, the reader may refer to *Ship Registries, Port of Eureka, California, 1859 to 1920* (1941) and Gibbs' *West Coast Windjammers* (1968).

Perhaps the most colorful history belonged to the *Wawona*, built in 1897 at the Bendixsen shipyard in Fairhaven for the Dolbeer and Carson Lumber Company. The evidence is that after a maiden voyage to San Diego the three-masted sailing vessel never again saw the waters of Humboldt Bay. Rather her immediate future was in loading fir from mills along Puget Sound for ports elsewhere. An article in the *Humboldt Historian* (May-June 1976, p. 8) refers to Carson's San Francisco correspondence as explaining why she was never used for the redwood trade. In the 1905 letter Carson states "we did not consider it possible for us to load her [;] she would probably come in right on top of the *Bertha* and *Azalea* and would no doubt have to lay up waiting for cargo [;] then the large amount she would carry would still further disturb the regular routine of filling our orders."

In 1913 the *Wawona* was sold and the new owners used her as a fishing boat to the Bering Sea. During World War II the United States government commandeered her as a lumber barge, sawing off the masts to deck level along with the bowsprit. After the war she was refitted as a fishing boat, which turned out to be financially unrewarding. Equally unsuccessful was the scheme for a share-the-cost cruise to the South Pacific. The vessel was then purchased by the movie star Gary Cooper and a partner for trade with Russia which failed to materialize. Eventually the *Wawona* came into the hands of sailing ship buffs who in the spring of 1975 moored the vessel at Marine Park in downtown Kirkland (near Seattle) as a museum relic open to the public. Certainly her lot would seem enviable compared to the fate of most schooners, swept away by storms at sea, destroyed by fire, or dismantled as obsolete hulks and the parts sold.

Carson disclosed the extensiveness and variety of their business ventures. To assure retail outlets for lumber the firm had acquired part interests in the San Pedro Lumber Company of Los Angeles and the San Diego Lumber Company. Then there were investments of capital in mills at Riverside, San Bernardino, and San Diego valued at $500,000. These mills did a widespread business in mouldings, sash doors, and house finishings. For diversification the two partners possessed oil land acreage in Ventura which was producing large quantities of coal oil. The *Times* (May 8, 1890) carries a story that a flow of 200 barrels daily was being recorded with prospects of an increased volume. For what it is worth, an interview with an old-timer suggested that the reason Carson left a more substantial estate than Dolbeer may be partly owing to the former buying up the latter's share in this venture and so reaping the subsequent greater profits. At any rate, Carson commented proudly that the lumber company held the highest standing in the commercial reports of Dun and Bradstreet. As its own postscript the *Standard* in the issue of December 31, 1883 observed that "Mr. Carson impresses one as a straight-forward, thoroughly practical, enterprising man. Everything about the mill and wharves of the company seem arranged with the utmost system and order. The whole aspect of the premises was indicative of good management, bearing an air of prosperity."

Local Personality

The task of making money did not rob Carson of a concern for his fellow men. He had the reputation of maintaining excellent relations with employees. He paid adequate wages and assisted them in personal crises. He kept them at work in slack periods and provided board at the cookhouse where the meals were described as rivaling those at hotels. There does not seem to be any record of suits for damages resulting from industrial accidents in which he was a defendant. On August 30, 1890, the eve of Labor Day, he voluntarily reduced working hours from twelve to ten. An article in the *Times* (September 2, 1890) described the gratefulness of the surprised mill hands. Accompanied by a band they marched to the Carson home and gave three hearty cheers for "their boss." Carson made an appearance on the porch and in response thanked them, noting it was only a measure of tardy justice six months late because of a vain effort to get the mill owners of Mendocino County to agree. Among those marching were employees from other mills, for the concession of Carson prompted other employers to follow suit. A further confirmation of his esteem with workers occurred in May 1907 when 2,000 loggers and mill hands went on strike for a closed shop, better wages, and improved working conditions. The Dolbeer and Carson Lumber Company remained unaffected, a testimony to the contentment of the men in his employ. And over the years, as the *Dolbeer and Carson Lumber Company Business Papers* (volumes 3 and 4, *passim*) record, Christmas money was distributed to employees, $5 for married men and $2.50 for single men.

Carson manifested an active interest in community enterprises. He was even ready to promote new industries, notably the Humboldt Bay Woollen Mills, which was generally regarded as successful. He helped launch the Humboldt Shoe Factory, purchasing three of the fifty shares, valued at $100 each, to provide the necessary capital. He joined in founding financial institutions, namely Humboldt County Bank, Bank of Eureka, and Savings Bank of Eureka. He served on their boards of directors and for a number of years was president of the Bank of Eureka. He participated in the formation of the North Mountain Power Company which later became the Western States Gas and Electric Company, and ultimately the Pacific Gas and Electric Company. When the local chamber of commerce was organized in 1883 he took out a membership and was named to its board of directors.

His identification with politics was at best modest. On several occasions, the earliest instance in 1864, he was elected as a trustee on the Eureka board of supervisors. According to Will N. Speegle, veteran newspaperman (*Times*, March 11, 1945), Carson once ran for the mayoralty but was defeated because of a railroad war and because the politicians were against him. On the state and national scene his allegiance was to the Republican Party; he accepted election as a delegate to the Republican County Committee in May 1875 and again in May 1886. It is quite possible that his second son, Charles Sumner, was named for the Republican senator from Massachusetts, for the family genealogy does not carry such a middle name for any member of the several generations of Carsons. That he retained his attachment to the Republican party might be deduced from an item in the *Standard* (October 14, 1897, p. 4a) announcing voluntarily a proposed increase in the wages of Dolbeer and Carson Company employees. Accompanying this welcome statement signalling an end to a lengthy period of depression in the lumber business was a comment with political overtones:

> "This notice was posted under the picture of [President William] McKinley, and is in line with a promise made by Mr. Carson last year, that if McKinley were elected, wages would be advanced. The amount of the raise is not stated in the notice but it will be a liberal one. The outlook for the lumber trade is good and prices are increasing. Mr. Carson says the McKinley tariff is responsible for the improvement and he believes that the hard times are over."

Carson was a member of Christ Episcopal Church and served as a vestryman throughout the span of his mature life. He is gratefully remembered in church histories for his generous financial support. He bought the land for the original site ($8,000) and annually helped to make up the deficits in the operating budgets. In his will he left the church a legacy of $20,000 which, with the accumulations in interest over the years, provided the nucleus for purchase of land for a new site at 625 Fifteenth Street and to erect the present beautiful Gothic structure. He was an equally active participant in the Humboldt Bay Mutual Relief Association (and at one time its president), contributing sums of money for charitable and humanitarian deeds. In his memoirs John Carr (1891, p. 425) submits an evaluation of Carson whom he knew personally first as a prospector for gold on the Trinity River and later as a fellow citizen of Humboldt County and a police judge in the city of Eureka:

> "Mr. Carson is a man of liberal ideals, always with a liberal hand helping our public institutions that are for the advancement of the people and the benefit of mankind. He is now President of the Bank of Eureka, and stands in the community as a man above reproach."

According to an annotated bibliography compiled by J. Carlyle Parker, one-time member of the library staff at Humboldt State University, the reputation acquired by Carson as an honorable businessman is supposed to be the basis for the novel by Peter B. (Bernard) Kyne entitled *The Valley of the Giants* (1919). If it will be recalled, three movies were filmed of this novel, all shot on locations in Humboldt County. The plot concerns the rivalry of two men for control of a proposed railroad line to haul logs. As an owner of timberlands the youthful hero, John Cardigan, opposes the monopolistic encroachments of a scheming lumber baron and rallies the community to give bitter resistance. In the end the good and righteous man triumphs over the ruthless and unscrupulous man. Certainly John Cardigan fits the description of Carson as an honest employer, scrupulous in business matters, and public-spirited. Kyne knew the country well, spent considerable time there, and undoubtedly was familiar with the personalities and events in the region. Indeed, Kyne worked for a while at Bay Mill and was among the employees remembered in Carson's will. The sum given him was $1,000 (*Dolbeer and Carson Lumber Company Business Papers,* volume 4, p. 339) and not $2,500 as the *Standard* (November 3, 1937) states in a related story. Kyne would appear to have resigned his job promptly and to have left for San Francisco to begin his career as a successful writer. Apparently one good turn deserved another when Kyne came to write his novel.

Carson married relatively late in life, in May 1864, at the age of thirty-eight. His bride, Sarah Wilson, came from his own birthplace, Charlotte County in the eastern Canadian province of New Brunswick. The wedding took place in San Francisco upon her arrival after a lengthy sea voyage "around the Horn" on the steamer *Golden City*. Perhaps it is this circumstance of their marriage in San Francisco which has led many writers to assume that she was a resident of that city. It is interesting to run across this news item in the *Weekly Humboldt Times* (July 20, 1861):

> "... William Carson left last week for a three months' visit Down 'East'. May he have a pleasant journey and kind greeting at home is the wish of all who know him and can appreciate the sterling qualities of an honorable man. It is whispered that William will not return a bachelor; this however needs confirmation."

Perhaps it was then that Carson had met his future wife and exchanged vows to be fulfilled as soon as his financial situation permitted. It might be added that according to notes in the *Fountain Papers* (volume 2, p. 00053) Sarah Wilson brought a brown wedding gown along with her.

Incidentally, on his travels in the east Carson wrote a letter to a Eurekan friend, J. M. Cox, dated August 15, 1861, from Niagara Falls, an extract of which was published in the *Weekly Humboldt Times* (October 5, 1861). Since it is the only personal letter known to the author, its verbatim inclusion might offer some degree of reality to Carson's personage. It should be remembered that the Civil War had broken out a few months previously and a military atmosphere prevailed. Presumably the passage was on the Great Lakes:

> "We [in company with a Eurekan, E. L. Whitney] left Aspinwall on the evening of the third of August on board the steamship *Champion* for New York. The same evening, about dark, there was considerable excitement created on board by the appearance of a low, black, suspicious looking steamer ahead of us about ten miles, lying directly across our track, and apparently awaiting our approach. So rather than run and risk, our Captain ordered the ship about and ran back to Aspinwall and reported to a man-of-war who got underway and went in search of the stranger. We also went to sea again the same night about ten o'clock. We saw nothing more exciting during the passage. We did not carry any lights as required by law during the passage, sailed on another route further to the eastward and gave the vessel we happened to see very wide berth.
>
> You recollect we heard that California steamers were well-armed; but I assure you the *Champion* had nothing but a few old rusty carbines, and two old cannons not fit to celebrate the Fourth of July with.... It is useless for me to write you concerning the war more than to say you cannot imagine the excitement that exists."

A postscript indicates that all cabin passengers including Carson signed a scathing letter addressed to Commodore (Cornelius) Vanderbilt, owner of the *Champion*, letting him know of his vessel's deficiencies.

To turn back to the union of William Carson and Sarah Wilson, there were four children born of the marriage, three sons and a daughter. In order of their birth they were John Milton (1865), Carlotta (1867), Charles Sumner (1873), and William Wilson (1877). Both John Milton and Charles Sumner married into locally prominent families. The former wed Mary Bell (Minnie) and the latter wed Amelia Ohman. William Wilson remained a bachelor. Carlotta married Robert James Tyson, a San Francisco marine insurance broker and subsequently a founder and one-time president of the Seaboard National Bank of San Francisco as well as a substantial investor in the Robert Dollar Steamship Company. Incidentally, in the *San Francisco Architectural Club Year Book* (1909, p. 44) among the building supply advertisements, there is a photograph of their home in the prestigious Piedmont district of Oakland. It is an imposing residence of three stories in Mediterranean style. One might speculate that Carlotta's father shared the cost as a belated wedding gift.

For William Carson the passage of years brought inevitable changes. In 1902 Dolbeer died but the company continued under its original name. William Wilson moved to San Francisco and took up the duties previously handled by Dolbeer. In May 1904 Mrs. Carson passed away at the age of seventy-one after a lengthy illness. The obituaries in the local newspapers lauded her as a woman of good heart and a ready spirit in charitable undertakings. On the day of her funeral the flags on the ships in the bay were at half mast and banks and businesses closed out of respect. It might be added that in the summer of 1904 Carson constructed a mausoleum on the family plot in Myrtle Grove Cemetery to care for members of the family and relatives in the future. Carson had three brothers and a sister and his wife had three sisters and a brother, most of whom had settled in Humboldt County. Later, in 1942, a year after the death of John Milton, the family crypts were moved to Sunset Memorial Park on the other side of town where a new cemetery had been laid out with more imposing and expansive grounds. There subsequent members of the second and third generations were allotted space.

William Carson himself, albeit sorrowed by the death of his wife, continued to thrive. In his article of 1904 David E. Gordon gives his impression of him as "still erect, elastic in movement, and unusually well-preserved." He stood six feet several inches tall and projected the image of a "man of the cloth" rather than a lumber magnate. Until within two months of his death, according to the *Times* (February 20, 1912), he could be seen daily walking into town. Photographs suggest an elderly gray-haired man of somber countenance and a face shrouded in a considerable greyish beard, after the manner of a venerable and august patriarch drawn from Biblical scenes. No doubt such a likeness of piety would have been highly prized by the devout Carson.

The esteem of William Carson in the community was never better evidenced than at the time of his death on February 19, 1912, at the age of eighty-seven, attributed to a severe cold which developed into pneumonia. On the day of his funeral, February 21, all businesses and public offices suspended activity from noon to four o'clock. An escort of 350 employees accompanied the body to the old Christ Episcopal Church. Over 2,000 people were reported as standing in the streets, unable to get into the church for the services and braving a cold wind. Afterwards the mourners proceeded to the Myrtle Grove Cemetery, a funeral cortege estimated at a half mile in length. The will as filed was published on the front page of the two local newspapers (February 27-28, 1912), a document described as covering seventeen typewritten pages and listing 116 beneficiaries, many of whom were company employees who received sums ranging from $1,000 to $15,000. Among charitable bequests were sums for the Episcopal Church at Elmsville, Charlotte County, New Brunswick, the Episcopal Trustees of Sacramento, and in San Francisco the Hospital for Children and Training Schools for Nurses, the Boys and Girls Aid Society, California's Women's Hospital, Florence Crittenden Home, and the Protestant Orphan Asylum. Reverend T. Shurtleff, rector of the Christ Episcopal Church in Eureka, was personally remembered with a bequest of $5,000. The entire estate was reckoned at more than $20,000,000, not an insignificant sum for those days.

Yet, notwithstanding this impressive array of surface facts, it is difficult to accept entirely the Christlike picture of his daily life. Whether or not he demurred at the excessive respect bestowed upon him, the prominence of his company and the wealth he had amassed must have been reflected in the human tendency of deference towards a "very important person." However modest he might have been and wanted to be, the retention of a sense of balance could have been very difficult. The probability would have been to look for leadership from him. Whether he exploited his standing in the community to force debatable views and actions is a matter of conjecture. Unfortunately he left no memoirs of any sort known to this writer. Nor is there available any collection of his spoken words. Only on very rare occasions in this manuscript will one find some words attributed to him or about him that suggest he was human after all. At the least, in the milieu of the nineteenth century, he could qualify as the better type of paternalistic benefactor. At the most, in the sense of human dignity, he could well have demonstrated the essence of democratic fellowship.

The Descendants

William Carson left the management of the lumber company in good hands. In 1911, one year before his death, he had turned over the business to his sons. In the *Dolbeer and Carson Lumber Company Business Papers* at Bancroft Library (vol. 4, March 1, 1911, p. 215) there appears the name of John Milton with the title of president. Where previously he had worked in the administrative office at $150 per month, he now received $300 per month and Charles Sumner the sum of $150 per month. John Milton assumed general responsibilities for production in Eureka while brother William Wilson continued to head the sales office in San Francisco. John Milton would appear also to have had good rapport with employees and to have observed the traditional practice of distributing gifts of money at Christmas time. The story is told that when the National Recovery Administration (N.R.A.) went into effect in 1933 at the behest of President Roosevelt, to promote voluntary agreements for dealing, among other things, with rates of pay, the company's wage scale was already in excess of the recommended base. Indeed, in the spring of 1935 when the local Lumber and Sawmill Workers Union called for a strike to procure collective bargaining, a thirty-hour week, and a minimum wage of seventy-five cents an hour, the mill crew at Dolbeer and Carson refused to join. The *Times* (May 12, 1935) carried on its front page the contents of a statement signed by the full complement of over 200 men for the attention of John Milton to the effect "that (1) we have always received the greatest of consideration from our president and friend Mr. J. M. Carson and do not need a union or any other organization to make demands for us and (2) we are fairly treated and have no complaints or grievances." Following this testimonial of loyalty, there was an acknowledgement by John Milton that "this list of names was unsolicited by me and represents 100% of the bay mill employees. None of the head men . . . or myself knew anything about it until the list was presented to me this morning [May 10]."

All three sons would seem to have handled well their inheritances, leaving large legacies upon their deaths—Charles Sumner (October 6, 1933), William Wilson (October 28, 1937), John Milton (August 25, 1941). The most numerous details are available for the will of William Wilson, published fully in the Eurekan newspapers a few days after his death in San Francisco. Apart from the bequests to relatives, the provisions recall the varied nature of his father's will. The employees of the Dolbeer-Carson Lumber Company were remembered with sums of money. The universities at Berkeley and Stanford were recipients for medical research and scholarships. Hospitals and churches in San Francisco were named in the will. The Christ Episcopal Church in Eureka was left $10,000, no doubt adding to the legacy left by his father for the erection of the new place of worship. In particular he stipulated $50,000 to the city of Eureka for a memorial to his father, a building erected at J and Harris Streets and known as the William Carson Memorial Community Center, which includes theatrical facilities. There are pictures of the father and the son in the entry hall as well as one of the mill crew from earlier decades. Close by, at H and Carson Streets, there is the Carson Park, two full blocks in a district of modest middle-class homes. It possesses a children's playground, a small hut office, restrooms, picnic tables, and open fields for sports, a very handy recreation area for a neighboring elementary school. Much of the money for this project came from funds in the William Carson Estate Company back in 1932.

The Carsons had four grandchildren—Sarah Bell and Marian by the marriage of John Milton Carson, and William Carson Tyson and Robert James Tyson, Jr. by the marriage of Carlotta. The Charles Sumner Carsons had no children. To follow the story of Carlotta's marriage (from official public records), it was dissolved on May 4, 1914. The charge of cruelty would seem rather unusual, the *Times* (May 5, 1914) carrying a small news item on the front page to the effect that Carlotta, "one of the wealthiest women in the west and member of a prominent Eureka family," alleged that her husband spoke disrespectfully of her father. Subsequently her ex-husband married Roberta Boyd, also of Piedmont, by whom he had one daughter by name Marie Tyson. That the divorce left overtones of bitterness was still evident when Robert J. Tyson (Sr.) died on October 13, 1921. His will gave his older son, William Carson Tyson, only "$1,000 and no more on account of the fact that he chose to live with his mother Carlotta C. Tyson, who is amply able to provide for him." His estate was appraised at $586,557.00, presumably his share of the divorce settlement under the community laws of the State of California. Carlotta C. Tyson died in San Francisco on April 10, 1932, her address given as 640 Sutter Street in San Francisco. Her will left an estate appraised at $633,081.56, the two children designated as the major heirs. In addition, it might be noted that the two Tyson boys received bequests from their uncle William Wilson Carson, Carlotta's brother.

Carlotta's sons seem to have gone off in different directions although apparently on very good terms. Both attended college briefly, William Carson on the campus at Berkeley in 1921 and Robert James, Jr. at Davis in 1929. At the time of his mother's death, Robert James, Jr. was listed as residing in Auburn, Placer County, California, a gold mining town some twenty miles northeast of Sacramento. Later he would appear to have become a resident of Honolulu. At the time of his death he was temporarily back in California for reasons of health. He died on November 28, 1944, at Colfax, also in Placer County, another twenty miles farther northeast of Auburn. Robert James, Jr. left no direct heirs, for his will, drawn up in Hawaii, gave his entire estate to his older brother. The latter and his wife, Irene (Hodgdon), remained in Piedmont for a while where he pursued the occupation of an insurance broker as had his father previously. Later the couple moved to southern California and settled in Solana Beach where William Carson Tyson became the owner of a fruit orchard. At the time of his death on November 26, 1968 his address had changed to La Jolla. A local obituary described him as seventy-one years of age and a resident of San Diego County for some thirty-two years, adding that he was a veteran of World War I and a member of a prominent Piedmont family. There were no children from this marriage and Mrs. William Carson Tyson died on May 23, 1978, at the age of eighty-eight years.

Both of the children of John Milton Carson married. Marian wed Sam Milton Haley, a member of the San Francisco stock exchange. Tragically, in March 1936, at the age of forty-three and plagued by illness,

Marian took her own life, a devastating blow to her parents, still living at the time. Sarah Bell married Clarence La Boyteaux of Fort Bragg, a coastal lumber community in Mendocino County. He eventually became superintendent of logging for the Dolbeer and Carson Lumber Company. They had one offspring, Ellsworth La Boyteaux, whose two daughters represent the fifth generation. Their center of habitation would seem to have been southern California, records indicating that Ellsworth had homes in Santa Barbara and Los Angeles. Whether there was much in the way of kinship visits between the La Boyteaux family and the Tysons is uncertain. However, the will of William Wilson Carson, youngest son of the lumber magnate, suggests close contacts for his bequests included his niece Sarah Bell La Boyteaux and his grand-nephew Ellsworth La Boyteaux, as well as the Tyson boys. Regrettably, efforts to contact Ellsworth La Boyteaux proved fruitless, for as the last direct descendant of the Carson family to live in the Carson Mansion his recollections would have been invaluable. At any rate, it would not be too much to say that the descendants of the Eurekan Carsons all sought life in the more bustling centers of sophistication.

CHAPTER THREE

CARSON MANSION: AN INTERPRETATION

Milieu

IT SHOULD NOT BE SUPPOSED that the Carson Mansion was designed in a cultural vacuum. Architecture no less than other arts is the product of historical circumstances. Kirker contends in *California's Architectural Frontier* (1960) that the rage for Gothic residences in the second half of the nineteenth century reflected the tensions and uncertainties inherent in post-Civil War society. The mass migration westward coupled with the renewed flood of immigrants from Europe challenged the stability of the nation. The bitter controversies over reconstruction in the south and the advent of the industrial revolution in the north added to the social turmoil and confusion in the country. At the same time the United States had sealed its political unity and faced the task of building a state of continental magnitude out of diverse peoples and sectional animosities. That the restlessness should filter down into the routine of everyday life is not surprising. As Maass describes it in *The Gingerbread Age* (1957), Americans indulged in extremes—heavy meals, strong drink, elaborate clothes, ornate furnishings, loud music, flowery speeches, thundering sermons.

One victim, if such it were, was the great promise of a pioneer architecture (perhaps the Spanish mission style on the Pacific coast) nourished by two decades of relative cultural isolation. But now the arts were cast loose from their traditional anchorage, to be tossed before the winds of self-conscious display. In America they manifested a tendency to drift away from their habitual acceptance as an integral part of the daily existence. Instead the arts shifted to become hardly more than a means to express prosperity and success in material achievements. Those whose fortunes were made sought their inspiration in the latest European trends. Apparently the sentimental and fanciful values of the romantic age abroad were a comfortable escape from the distressing realities of a divided nation. The marvels of medieval castles and cathedrals were rediscovered. The popularity of Sir Walter Scott's novels and the collection of picturesque drawings and engravings testified to the new fashions. So the opulent man of the world and his imitators dressed up their homes in the borrowed finery of historic modes albeit often strangely scrambled. But that did not matter so long as the results were either striking or quaint.

California was no exception and found itself swept into the maelstrom of personal ambition, extravagant taste, and Byzantine indulgence. Most of the wealthy men were *nouveaux riches,* garnering their fortunes in gold and silver mines, timberlands, railroads, utilities, and cattle. The architectural development of the Golden State took its lead from the eastern seaboard where imports from the European scene captured the day. Men like Leland Stanford, Charles Crocker, Collis Potter Huntington, and Mark Hopkins led the way and their palatial homes in San Francisco were the envy of a burgeoning high society. But the Gothic Revival style which emerged along the Atlantic coast was not exactly that adopted on the Pacific coast. Where the former recreated in stone its counterparts of the Gothic age, the latter sought refuge in wooden motifs. Whatever the reasons—costliness and lack of competent stonemasons—the availability of wood and the alchemy of the jigsaw dictated the tracery of the Gothic structure in the west. Indeed, many believe that California surpassed the rest of the country in its imaginative application of such features. However critical were the references to its sham substantiality and artistic disarray, the product could be both wondrous and exotic. The bizarre designs refused to countenance a plane surface or a continuous line, perhaps a tribute to the exuberance of the intrepid pioneers confident of a glorious national destiny now that the country had been emancipated from the incubus of slavery.

Some observations with regard to terminology seem in order. For one thing, the word Victorian means simply architectural prototypes during the reign of Queen Victoria borrowed from previous centuries, but nothing distinctive enough to claim originality for her decades. For a second thing, many architects repudiate the word "style" and refuse to recognize the realities claimed for it. Baird in *Time's Wondrous Changes* (1962) offers the word "fashion" as an alternative. If this dichotomy of thought among the professionals be fully understood, it is surely not harmful to use either term as a convenient point of departure. The vital fact is that the architect secured for himself a considerable degree of latitude to meet the individual desires of a client. Although rooted in the medieval past, the Gothic Revival as it evolved in America emerged adulterated with details and features labeled Italian, French, Tudor, Elizabethan, and even Oriental. Some writers prefer the nomenclature of Victorian Eclecticism, listing as varieties Bracketed Gothic, Rural Castellated, Pointed or Tudor, Old English, Italian Villa, Elizabethan, and Rustic Pointed. More often the classifications have been boiled down to Italianate, French Accent, Stick, Eastlake, and Queen Anne, identified by such landmarks as the roof lines, cornices, towers, brackets, gables, porticoes, and windows In the case of California, to paraphrase Lyle F. Perusse, listed as a reference librarian at the University of California, Los Angeles, the Gothic approach from 1850 to 1890 mirrored in microcosm a cavalcade of American palatial homes (and buildings).

Architectural Historians

The identification of the architectural style of the Carson Mansion has had a wide range of interpretations. Maass includes the Eurekan residence in his chapter on the French Accent, a reference to the period of the Second Empire during which Napoleon III reigned. Its hallmark is the mansard or double-pitch roof, originally devised to permit a full story to be accommodated under the eaves and so avoid taxation for additional stories. By manipulating the roof line downward more interior space is allowed for living quarters compared to the cramped attic of a peaked roof. Obviously a mansard house could not have less than two stories and most had three stories for the needs of the usually large Victorian family. A mansard roof has four sides broken for light and ventilation by projecting dormer windows. As applied in America (and illustrated graphically by the initial buildings on the Berkeley campus of the University of California) the classic French roof could be convex or concave or twisted into an exuberant S-shape. At the bottom and top of the slopes there are strongly-marked cornices for the curbs, the lower resting upon bold brackets and the upper featuring iron cresting. In the case of the Carson Mansion the multiplicity of gables and the rich application of ornamentation would seem to diminish any identifiable characteristics of the Second Empire style save for a sort of mansard roof in the tower portion.

Wesley Vail, an active professional in city planning in San Francisco and Sonoma County with an avowed interest in the preservation of nineteenth century Gothic architecture dwells upon the penetrating influence of the Italianate in the exterior of the Carson Mansion. Both the initial edition of his book in 1964 carrying as its main title *Victorians* and in the revised second edition of 1978 with the altered title *San Franciscan Victorians* are concerned with the period from 1870 to 1890. He regards "the basic matrix for much of San Francisco victorian design" as the Italian style, albeit in the case of the Carson Mansion in Eureka "it [emerged] later in a disguised form." For illustrations of his thesis he includes the familiar front elevation sketch along with several black and white photographs—a twentieth century front profile, a close-up of the tower, an angle profile of the porch and second story. Later in the book on the subject of Victorian interiors one encounters the equally familiar photographs of the entry hallway and the scene from the head of the second floor hallway.

The Italian-flavored poems of Robert and Elizabeth Browning did much to popularize the villa in England. The royal couple, Queen Victoria and Prince Albert, added to its popularity by commissioning Osborne House on the Isle of Wight in the villa style. As transplanted to the American continent the early ones were known as Tuscan villas from their Florentine origin. These square-towered houses had such classic features as a flat front facade, with a light cornice line and simple pediments over windows and doors. They might possess columned porticoes, railed balconies, roof bracketry, and arched paired windows. The more familiar style by the 1870s might be called High Victorian Italianate. The profile became more irregular, although retaining the classicized Corinthian columns, a central front porch, tall and narrow windows, and a flat and heavily-bracketed roof line. But the windows were more often dressed with segmented arches or broken pediments, set in double-tiered and angled bays, and flanked with colonnettes. The entrance porches rippled with fluted columns, turned balustrades, and considerable ornamentation. The roof could be slightly pitched, gabled or hipped, and have a wide overhang with the eaves supported by overscaled brackets, thus lending itself to shadow-forming mouldings and a diversity of openings. The square tower aloft the structure might be centered or stand off at a corner. This lookout was called a cupola or belvedere, reached by a trap door, and topped by a scrolled finial which could form the base of a flagpole or a weather vane. No doubt grist could be gathered by those who saw much of the Italianate, especially the tower, in the Carson Mansion.

What distinguished Stick-Eastlake and Queen Anne from the other styles was the total commitment to wood for the structural framework, exterior walls, roof, and decorative ornamentation. The progenitor was industrial technology—the lathe, the circular saw, and the bandsaw replaced the chisel and the gouge. Carving and turning which for centuries past had been the province of the highly skilled hand craftsman now gave way to steam powered (and later electrically operated) woodworking machinery. The relative ease with which such modern equipment could manipulate the wood fed to it encouraged architects, builders, and decorators to indulge in miscellaneous, exotic, and bewildering designs. It made possible an endless number of what might well be called a ballet in pirouettes, arabesques, and attitudes—rabbiting, mitering, jointing, beveling, squaring, smoothing, cornering, tapering, halfing, fluting, panel raising, waved moulding, and circular, oval, and elliptical dovetailing. Local carpenters and mills exercised their ingenuity in imaginative shapes of scrolls and curlicues to an extent that the result is often described as Carpenters' Gothic.

Kirker in an essay entitled "California Architecture and Its Relation to Contemporary Trends in Europe and America" (1973) leaned towards the Stick interpretation of the Carson Mansion. He traced the origin back to the wood building tradition in Northern Europe over the past several hundred years. Followers of European architectural trends on the eastern coast and in the midwest took up the technique for their homes. As adapted on the Pacific coast, it assumed an American cast by combining the "balloon frame construction" with a simplified "Gothic-Swiss" stylistic formula. It may be described as a light frame of studs (two-by-four) and plates nailed together, with the advantages of requiring less wood than the old jointed frames, less time to erect, and lending itself to more flexible building plans. But the Stick design soon became enmeshed in a fantasy of Second Empire, Eastlake, and Queen Anne components. In San Francisco's ebullient "champagne days," the Stick style acquired a mansard roof, the sharply incised Eastlake ornamentation, and the helter-skelter surface of shingles described as more "Mary-Anne than Queen Anne." The acceptance of Stick was quite logical in regions of alternating fog and sunshine charged with strong contrasts of light and shadows. Such conditions proved ideal for the propagation of Stick whose character depended upon the projected structural members throwing their filtered reflections across the surface of the buildings. In this respect the least inhibited projection of the Stick was the bay window with its billowing sheets of glass enclosed in whimsically-ornamented frames and crowned with pierced entablatures and bracketed pediments.

Elinor Richey, writer and lecturer on architectural preservation, in *Remain To Be Seen* (1973) referred to the Carson Mansion as containing an admixture of Stick-Eastlake. The unwilling innovator was an English architect by the name of Charles Eastlake whose interests were primarily with the functional reform of furniture. He would woo the public away from curvaceous French influences to straight, squared-off and flat-surfaced furniture but embellished with floral and geometric designs. His eager followers, however, extended his ideas and added them to the new "Stick" architectural style. They would apply his incised ornamentation on the exteriors in variegated patterns. Crisscrossed strips were laid on plane surfaces in the manner of Elizabethan half-timbering. English foliation under the western sun crept over exteriors like a tropical vine. The facade became a huge wood mosaic, regarded as burlesque by Eastlake, already irritated by the use of his name for the unseemly concoctions. But proponents of Stick-Eastlake argued that the shingled frame construction and its ornamentation expressed truly the character of the natural surroundings. In the way of details, the exterior walls were faced in combinations of horizontal sidings and vertical boards and battens. An elaborate configuration of turned and beveled wood artistry enhanced pillars, doors, corner plates, and bargeboards. Indeed, the credence of the visuals must have been strained by the scrolls and curlicues crowding the supportive posts of porches and verandas and the exposed members of the roof. The most sophisticated residences of this kind usually had steep roofs, eaves of considerable projections, and sturdy brackets. No doubt an imaginative observer could readily spot many of the familiar fantasies of Stick-Eastlake in the Carson Mansion.

If Gebhard conceded that there was a little bit of every style to be discerned in the Carson Mansion, he regarded it as overall in the category of Queen Anne. He described the evolving creation as an English import, developing from Elizabethan and Tudor representations commingled with such Dutch influences as accompanied the reign of William III (and Mary). He would define it "as any eccentricity in general design that one can suppose would have occurred to designers 150 to 200 years ago." In California the term came to cover indiscriminately a multitude of work that would defy positive classification. The American version with its substitution of wood and shingles for brick and tile emphasized the picturesque rather than the historical elements. The designs adjusted readily to the balloon frame method of construction. The stress placed upon the Queen Anne style for the Carson Mansion was repeated by Gebhard and his coworker Harriette Von Breton during the celebration of the centennial anniversary of the University of California. On the campus of the Santa Barbara branch, from April 16 to May 12, 1968, they organized an architectural exhibition of significant California structures. A catalogue was published providing both texts and photographs of the leading examples over the one-hundred year span. The familiar front elevation sketch of the Carson Mansion exterior drawn by the architects was included in the catalogue. One copy I used was borrowed from John D. Henderson, a San Diego architect prominent in local endeavors to preserve places of historic interest. What made his copy doubly interesting was the fact that he had pencilled-in his interpretations of stylistic features attached to the buildings and residences shown. He rated the Carson Mansion a high point in the Queen Anne style and stressed the proliferation of the gingerbread details as a focal feature.

Russell Lynes, member of the Society of Architectural Historians and one-time managing editor of *Harper's Magazine,* offers a more precise description of what constituted the exterior of a Queen Anne house in a book entitled, *The Domesticated Americans* (1957, p. 101):

> It frequently has an octagonal or round tower at one of its corners that face the street. Its veranda is wide and its railings are spindled. Its roof is long, sharply pitched, and pierced with peaked dormers, and its chimneys are frequently in shapes borrowed from Elizabethan country houses. Its several upstairs balconies are characteristically recessed into the house and sheltered by eaves.

The medieval Gothic world thus reconstructed was a poetic conception, mysterious but fresh. The profile was irregular, each facade having a different elevation. The multiple-gabled roof was high and possessed of a precipitous slant, with its intersecting ridges at right angles ignoring solid geometry. Both dormer and oriel windows were popular and the variations in the elevations permitted a maximum of sunlight. Wherever space allowed on the facade there were injections of Stick-Eastlake ornamentation such as sham half-timbering, fancy-cut shingles, and corner towers topped with a pointed dunce cap or bulging helmet. The Queen Anne blueprint was very accommodating and offered something to please everyone's taste—high-peaked roofs, chimneys, bargeboards (vergeboards), spindled verandas, and stained glass windows. Paradoxical as it might seem, some architects contend this busy pattern created a unity of its own, very much like a patchwork quilt composed of assorted fabrics. Certainly the Queen Anne style represented a delightful insurrection against monotony, an asymmetrical arrangement of almost endless variety. One can easily conjure up the opportunity for priority claims relative to the Carson Mansion between the two styles of Stick-Eastlake and Queen Anne.

It might be of interest to match Gebhard's appraisal of the Carson Mansion with Baird's data book report (1964):

> "... The principal entrance faces west and the general design of the house is oriented to this view. In type, the Carson House is a Stick-Villa... such as the present Governor's Mansion in Sacramento of 1877. The loft, more or less off-center tower and picturesque massing are characteristic of the later Villas of nineteenth century American architecture.... One can see interest in stick or strip articulation—so common in California houses of the 1880's. Reduplicated strips frame

the corners of the vertical rhythms from story to story. Most of the upper exterior wall surfaces have variations on shingle patterns—either of an undulant type or a more scale-like type (the latter especially characteristic of the later 1880's). With its grotesquely steep gables and delayed Victorian Gothic bargeboards, the house reflects that interest in medievalizing forms which produced Stick, Single and Queen Anne designs. (Rounded towers at the rear of the Carson House also suggest Queen Anne.) There are, of course, some 'original' decorative features which make this house virtually unique. In general, architects of the period drew upon sixteenth century Mannerist sources without always realizing what they were doing. The bulbous, out-sized, eccentric 'spindle' pillars of the principal porch which encircles the west and south sides of the house, the bizarre broken and canted pediment over the main stair, and the extremely tall, constructed feeling of ornamental parts—this is Mannerist. The exact source is more easily seen as Eastlake patterns modified by an interest in later sixteenth century English and Italian details; but the end result is a special mixture which is grandiosely hideous in the inspired manner of certain Roman 'follies' of the sixteenth century...."

Newsom Brothers, Architects

The Newsom brothers, architects for the Carson Mansion, need to be rescued from comparative oblivion. Indeed, an overdue recognition of their architectural achievements was held in the form of an exhibition with catalogue by Gebhard, at the University of California, Santa Barbara, in the spring of 1979 (and then repeated at the Oakland Museum). In the meanwhile he had written an introduction to a reprint of the first pattern book co-authored by Samuel and Joseph Cather in 1884 (published in October 1978) which has been very useful in completing this subsection. From correspondence with Samuel Newsom, Jr., a grandson of Samuel, and S. D. Nelson, a grandson of Joseph Cather, Gebhard has pieced together the biographical facts related to the family which arrived in San Francisco in the early eighteen-sixties. They soon settled in Oakland where the father came to operate a nursery to complement his interest in horticulture. The pertinent point for us is that there were four sons, the two older brothers—John J. and Thomas D.—destined to form a partnership as architects, just as the two younger brothers did in the course of time.

The respective ages of Samuel and Joseph Cather are in some degree disputable. According to the obituaries for Samuel in the *San Francisco Chronicle* (September 2, 1908) and the *Architect and Engineer* (September

1908, p. 79), they were natives of Toronto, Canada, Samuel being listed as eight years old at the time of their arrival in California. But these accounts differ as to his age upon death, the former citing it as 56 years and the latter as 61 years. According to the *Oakland Tribune* (June 5, 1930), Joseph Cather was 72 years old at the time of his death. In any instance, the available data would indicate that Joseph Cather was the younger brother. For what it is worth, the *Great Register, County of Alameda, 1884* carries the information that Samuel at the time of citizenship (July 28, 1875) was 23 years of age and Joseph Cather (February 8, 1879) 21 years of age, which works out as an age difference of some six years, a figure arrived at likewise by Gebhard. Both made Oakland their home although they established offices in San Francisco and Los Angeles as well. Each left families upon their demise, Samuel being survived by a wife, four sons, and two daughters, and Joseph Cather by a wife, one son, and one daughter.

Both Samuel and Joseph Cather served an apprenticeship under their eldest brother John J. Directories for the local region (particularly Langley's and Bishop's) provide the information that in 1873 Samuel was a draftsman in the office of John J. However, by 1879, the two younger brothers had formed a partnership, for in the July issue of that year the *Quarterly Architectural Review* lists building contracts being undertaken by S. and J. C. Newsom. Quite mystifying is the dissolution of their partnership, chronicled by Gebhard as in January 1888. Samuel continued in San Francisco and Oakland in association with two sons, Sidney and Noble (who were joined by a third brother, Archie, after the demise of their father). Joseph Cather remained in Los Angeles where he had been managing the firm's extensive southern California operations. The reader may find photographs and brief descriptions of houses he designed in Gebhard and Winter, *A Guide to Architecture in Los Angeles and Southern California* (1977). After the collapse of the building boom in Los Angeles, Joseph Cather moved about frequently, spending an interim period as far away as Philadelphia. He returned permanently to Oakland by 1900 and became an active architect once more, as a perusal of the monthly issues of the *California Architect and Building News* (successor to the *Quarterly Architectural Review*) will testify. His drawings and sketches of house plans were featured often in this journal, no less than those of Samuel. As a feather in his cap he served on the California State Board of Architecture for successive two-year terms from 1907 to 1919. Thereafter he is no longer listed as a certified architect and he would appear to have been engaged in real estate, for in the *Oakland Realtor* (August 21, 1923), the published roster of the Oakland real estate board so carries him.

Regardless of their personal relations, the prestigious structures attributed to Samuel and Joseph Cather are reflective of the eclecticism which characterized their careers. In the case of the Oakland city hall (1869) and the Alameda County courthouse (1875), the degree of credit to be apportioned presents a dilemma for the historian. The family of Joseph Cather saw fit in his obituary to claim for him a role in their construction. Apart from both appearing to have been rather young for such achievements, assuming that Samuel was born in 1852 and Joseph Cather in 1858, the evidence seems otherwise as to their authorship. The *Oakland Daily Transcript* (June 8-25, 1869) follows the squabble over the performance of Olney, the architect selected for the city hall and never a mention of the Newsoms. Perhaps a later addition or renovation, for the building was badly damaged by fire in 1877, may have involved them, but certainly not the original design. As for the Alameda County courthouse, the *Oakland Daily News* (June 26, 1874) simply states that it is "the work of Newsom Brothers who rank among the best architects in the State." Considering the chronology, the reference might well mean the older two brothers. The most that might be said for the younger two brothers was some responsibility for the designs as draftsmen.

At any rate, there can be no mistaking the eclectic quality of all four brothers in architectural designs. Drawings and photographs of the Alameda County courthouse (as well as of the Oakland city hall) are available in several local histories. The Alameda County courthouse was located on Broadway and Fourth Streets in Oakland. At a distance in profile it looms overall as Second French Empire (as was the smaller Oakland city hall) with sub-style features. The first and second story windows have the familiar Italianate look—tall, angular, and arched at the top. Corinthian columns ornament the front facade and support the cornice work. The mansard roof is broken into, surrounded as it is by triangular pediments and circular parapets. The third floor, cased by the mansard roof, possesses the usual projecting dormer windows. Above the roof lines a massive cupola soars, enveloping a tower in the manner of a pavilion and capped with a finial.

That the versatility of Samuel Newsom himself broadened over the years is testified to by his victorious commission for the Agricultural and Horticultural Hall in connection with the California Midwinter International Exposition held in 1894. The director-general of this gala event was Michael Harry de Young, publisher of the *San Francisco Chronicle*, and for whom later the M. H. de Young Memorial Museum in Golden Gate Park was named. His promotion of the fair was partly to offset a business recession and partly to advertise the mild California winter in contrast to the snow and cold experienced in most sections of the nation. An interesting description of Newsom's winning creation may be found in a souvenir program published by H. S. Crocker company, San Francisco, in its Educational Series (No. 2, May 14, 1894). The commentary opposite the beautifully-colored drawing of the building calls it "a combination of the Spanish Mission (separate towers and domes), the Romanesque (arched low entrances), and the Moorish (decorative features)." The account goes on to note that the low sloping red roof lines are overshadowed in the center by a huge glass dome to show off the floral arrangements being exhibited on the main floor.

The laudatory reviews must have been very gratifying to Samuel Newsom. One of the self-labeling official guides regarded "the low yet graceful arches, spreading roof, minor domes and towers... as an example of all that is most beautiful in the old museum buildings,... one of the most notable of the Exposition edifices." The main entrance "is formed by a beautifully proportioned arch,... supported by two columns, forming three minor arched ways leading into a vestibule opposite the rotunda beneath the dome... [and] the frieze is quaintly decorated with child figures [sort of Kate Greenaway figures in bas-relief from which he may well have gotten his inspiration]." The *California Architect and Building News* (August 1893) commended him, for while the "foundation of his work is the Mission,... he used his own ideas to adapt to the requirements of the building and cannot be considered a servile copy of any order of architecture.... The Great Dome is a striking feature, 101 feet, 6 inches in diameter and 90 feet high from ground to 'Lantern.'" Equally congratulatory was the official catalogue published by Harvey, Whitcher, and Allen (1894), passing on the observation that "Newsom happily [adopted] the ideas of the Mission Fathers and the single break is the huge glass dome seen from all parts of the Fair Grounds."

No less impressive are the two structures designed by Samuel Newsom for the St. Louis Fair of 1904 commemorating the centenary of the Louisiana Purchase. The reader is referred to the articles, with drawings and photographs, in the *Sunset Magazine* (September 1903, p. 493, April 1904, pp. 481-484, September 1904, pp. 405-411). The contribution of the city of San Francisco was a reproduction of the Union ferry depot, scaled down considerably. In profile it may be described as Roman Revival, featuring Corinthian columns and semicircular tracery windows. A square-shaped campanile is centered to the rear of the building and supports a series of classical pavilions terraced one above the other and capped by a cupola. The California state building was a reproduction of the Mission Santa Barbara and is described as a representative revival of the neoclassic restoration style of the 1950s. The solid and massive wall is graced by a triangular pediment and three Ionic columns on each side of the arched entrance. At each end above the roof line there rises a square bell tower (double-tiered) with dome and lantern. The facade, however, manifests a variation from the original, possessing a large circular window balanced by two small circular windows one on each side, all often alluded to as "exterior reveals." In contrast the Mission Santa Barbara possesses one small circular window along with a larger one, the latter perhaps symbolically a Rose Window much like that at Chartres. As for the two-story annexes extending out on the wings, the lower floor presents a continuity of arcaded cloisters and the upper floor a continuity of square openings, the result assuring the faithful ample corridors for a cool promenade.

For the rest, an article in the *World's Fair Bulletin* (September 1903) would delve further back in history for Newsom's architectural inspiration of the California state building, calling it "a replica of the famous old La Rabida Mission," a venerable Franciscan friary (close by the port of Huelva on the coast facing the Gulf of Cadiz) and reputed to have been the locale where Christopher Columbus worked out the plans for his Atlantic sailing. For a photograph (which would suggest, however, that the Mission Santa Barbara is much more the prototype) see Ernle Bradford, *Christopher Columbus* (1973, p. 61).

If the varied architectural styles employed by the Newsoms in public buildings stamp the eclectic quality of their approach, they were especially enthusiastic in the embracement of the Gothic Revival. In this respect it would not be too much to say that they were a major influence in spreading the gospel of the "picturesque." The recent revised second edition of Vail's book devotes considerable space to their leadership. One need only to leaf through the pages of the *California Architect and Building News* for many examples of their ability to translate the trend into reality. The Carson Mansion, of course, has been the basis for whatever reputation has managed to linger on. In numbers their commissions were endless, estimated by Gebhard at over 600 buildings. In their first pattern book the Newsom brothers described themselves as "publishers, architects, and superintendents, prepared to go to any part of the State." While the San Francisco Bay region provided the locale for the bulk of their contracts, the commissions carried them to such communities as San Rafael, Los Gatos, Petaluma, Healdsburg, Napa, Pinole, San Jose, Santa Clara, Centerville, Stockton, Santa Rosa, and Eureka. Among the credits may be listed Highland Park College in East Oakland, the Second United Presbyterian Church and the First English Evangelical Lutheran Church in San Francisco, and the First Presbyterian Church in Berkeley. Gebhard and Von Breton have a few additional ones in the published catalogue related to the exhibition held in 1968 at the University of California (Santa Barbara) which covered a century of California architecture. These included the Bradbury House in Los Angeles, the Glendale Hotel in Glendale, and the Town Hall in Gilroy.

An interesting story involved the conception of Samuel Newsom as to what would be an appropriate design for a governor's mansion in Sacramento. He labeled his sketch "Un Chateau En Espagne," to be built in Spanish style of red stone with a tile roof. Included were such sub-style features as a mansard roof with dormer windows, bargeboards richly decorated, a triple-arched entrance, round turrets, and finials. The commentary of the *California Architect and Building News* (February 1891) was friendly, welcoming "Samuel Newsom's idea of the kind of gubernatorial residence the State should build for our Chief Executive [and] we hope that the future will bring a realization of such a public building for the purpose intended." As it turned out, however, the State of California purchased in 1903 a private residence on Sixteenth and H Streets for the governor's mansion, appropriately a classic model of the Gothic Revival built back in 1877 and referred to by Baird as "Stick Villa."

William Carson is supposed to have given the Newsoms a free hand and if this is true some discussion of their architectural views should set the stage for the Eurekan adventure. To that end there are four pattern books (or volumes as they are often listed), all available in the flesh at Bancroft Library. The reader should be aware that the publications are undated and the entries in such catalogues as those of the University of California at Berkeley and Los Angeles and the National Union Catalog Pre-1956 Imprints range from "1884-9?" to "circa 1884" and "1890-1893?" Each of the first two pattern books has as its title, *Picturesque California Homes,* and is co-authored by Samuel and Joseph Cather Newsom. By the use of internal and external evidence Gebhard chronicles correctly the first volume as issued in 1884 or early 1885 and the second volume in 1887. The third and fourth volumes are the work of Joseph Cather and as such must have been issued after the dissolution of the partnership in 1888. The third volume is entitled, *Picturesque and Artistic Homes and Buildings in California,* and issued in 1890 as actually stated on the outside cover. The fourth volume is entitled *Modern Homes of California,* with the generally acceptable date of publication as 1893, to be deduced from the comment by Joseph Cather (p. 19) fixing "the progress in the past two or three years [since volume 3] as marked and noticeable."

The presence of the word "picturesque" in the title of three of the four volumes suggests an acquaintance with the writings of Andrew Jackson Downing, the American apostle of Gothic ornateness. Each of the volumes includes advice on the selection of an architect, basic construction principles, and a collection of house plans. Where in the first two volumes the plates are drawings, the last two volumes contain also photographs. The cost of each volume ranged from $2.50 for the paper bound and $5.00 for the cloth edition (compared to $14.95 for the recent "quality paperback" reprint), with some revenue being derived from the advertisements. That

Joseph Cather regarded himself as the progenitor of all four volumes may be drawn from a statement in volume 3 (p. 23), referring "readers to consult my Volume No. 1 published about seven years ago and then Volume 2 issued some four years since...." That this might be a hint of a lingering bitterness in the dissolution of the partnership is strengthened by the fact that in volumes 3 and 4 Joseph Cather called attention to the reproduced photographic illustrations as carefully selected from the work of the "Leading Architects in different parts of the State." Then he went on to list about a dozen specific firms including himself but not his brother Samuel.

Apropos the obvious rift in the relations of the two Newsom brothers, neither seemed prepared to rest individual laurels on the four-volume set of pattern books. Joseph Cather published what would appear an interim declaration of his own worth during his stay in Los Angeles. It is entitled *Artistic Buildings and Homes of Los Angeles,* comprising twenty photographs of residences and businesses which he inferred had been designed by himself, including the well-known Bradbury home. The price was $1.00 and carried the usual complement of building supply advertisements. It may be chronicled as issued in 1888-1889 based upon the statement of a Los Angeles bank which listed its financial condition as of July 1, 1888.

Much more impressive in size and depth was the pattern book published by Samuel entitled *Some City and Suburban Homes*. The price was $3.50 and it numbered one hundred pages which included some fifty full size and scale drawings of mostly house plans and were profusely interspersed with building supply advertisements. It may be chronicled as issued in 1890 based upon a) one firm announcing its new location as from July 1, 1890 and b) an insurance company listing its assets as of November 30, 1889. Samuel offered, as had the previously co-authored pattern books, a description of the latest styles in interior decorations. As for the several pages detailing the highlights of his plans and bearing his signature, the fact that they represented homes in specific California communities could well infer a consciousness of his own creativity. Be these surface summaries of these two pattern books as they may, the relevant point is that the exteriors profiled show that their approach still accented the varieties of Gothic Revival and contribute to the following analysis of the Newsoms' architectural views.

The Newsoms stressed that the advances in house building on the eastern coast did not meet the needs of the Californians. The urgency to keep out snow, ice, and extreme cold were not problems in the Golden State. Instead of structures utilizing brick and stone in heavy and massive styles, a wood exterior providing a more open way of living would suffice. The object was to mold all styles of architecture known to the ages and adapt them to the local environment. The product must satisfy "the dictates of comfort, please the eye, and [be] peculiarly graceful and so peculiarly Californian." Their list of characteristic points included verandas, balconies, porches, gables, pediments, "to be thrown in where least expected, thereby adding to the uniqueness of design." They fancied redwood shingles oiled, varnished, stained, or painted. Where required, bay windows in round, octagon, or square shapes could be run in. Such bay windows, together with towers surmounting them and finished out with iron and gilded finials, should make a very imposing profile. Overall the exterior should be shingled from water tables to eaves for a rural and original effect. In terms of Gothic Revival styles, the Newsoms described their many creations as "Picturesque Cottage," "Swiss Combination," "Queen Anne," "Eastlake," and "Modernized Queen Anne."

In the way of exterior painting combinations, the Newsoms submitted a variegated set of color schemes to secure the picturesque theme. Some of those listed they had used and others they had seen used. What strikes one is the inexhaustible vocabulary of color concocted for visual effect, a sensuosity rivaled today only by the assaults of a Disneyland or the graffiti in New York subways:

"Base pompeian red, body olive green, with trimmings on body bronze green, underneath cornice terra cotta, roof venetian red and black, or dark brown chimney, striped black on venetian red ground, sash Indian red,... front [and] side doors and vestibules grained mahogany....

Body maroon, trimmings seal brown, sash ash yellow, roof dark brown, base dark Indian red, vestibule in oak.

Two shades of brown (light seal and dark seal brown) roof dark brown, chimneys dark brown, chimneys dark terra cotta, plain colors, soffit of cornice or underneath cornice sky-blue or robin-egg blue, roof slate color....

Chimneys were pressed brick and oiled, ceilings of veranda robin-egg blue, steps granite, sash bronze green, railings black...."

Certainly there is no one more qualified to expound upon the architectural technique of the Newsoms than Gebhard, and excerpts from his analysis in the introduction to the reprint of the first pattern book by the brothers merit quotation (with due acknowledgement to Hennessey and Ingalls, Inc., Los Angeles, publishers of this re-issue in 1978):

"... Their earliest work could be characterized as loosely Eastlake, which was followed by designs in all of the major styles of the 80s, 90s and early 1900s—the Queen Anne, Richardsonian Romanesque, the Chateauesque, and the Colonial Revival Shingle style. By the early 90s, Samuel and Joseph Cather became interested in designing in the regionally developed Mission Revival style [as witness the designs of Samuel for the expositions held in San Francisco in 1894 and in St.

Louis in 1904]. Later came designs . . . in the Spanish Colonial Revival and even the Pueblo Revival. Side by side with designs employing regional images, they created others which were classical and Beaux Arts, Gothic and English Tudor, and after 1900 often Craftsman-bungalow and late Shingle style. . . .

.. ..

Though they kept up with the latest styles, . . . perhaps the most telling element in their work was the peculiar way in which they mixed and maneuvered their details and forms. They both seem to take a delight in seizing upon a detail and then enlarging it, or miniaturizing it, and then posing it not as an integrated feature of a design but as a separate, highly individual historic fragment. From beginning to end their designs were (from the point of view of sophisticated academic architecture) an affront. There was always something bizarre—and therefore delightful and playful—about their buildings. For the trained architect or critic, their designs are almost always outrageous, and yet the outrageousness is so appealing that we tend to be won over."

In this connection, this being a convenient place to insert an interesting and closing vignette, one might take note of the home given by William Carson in 1889 to his eldest son, John Milton, as a wedding gift. Gebhard writes in the co-authored *Guide to Architecture in San Francisco and Northern California* (1973, p. 322) that while it was overshadowed by his father's home across the street, "it contains the full vocabulary of the Newsoms when they were working in the Queen Anne style, [especially beautiful are] the stained glass windows off the front porch." There is a round turret at one corner of the house and considerable gingerbread about the bargeboards and windows along with the ever picturesque fish scales on the exterior frame. Regrettably my inquiry as to which Newsom had been the architect brought the response from the present owner, Robert Madsen, a local realtor, that the building permits of the previous century had not been retained in the county archives. But one may presume that Samuel received the contract, considering that Joseph Cather was probably still engaged in winding up his affairs in the Los Angeles area.

The pink and white combination which is now the color scheme for the exterior has won for the residence its distinction as "Pink Lady." After Milton moved into his deceased father's mansion he sold the vacated house. A placard posted by the front door for the edification of tourists tells the subsequent story. Over the years the ownership changed hands several times and eventually was bequeathed to two sisters residing in Germany. Their decision was to operate the residence as a lodging house. In 1942 the United

States government seized the premises as Nazi property and later sold it at public auction in 1951 to Lloyd Bridges and associates (father of the movie-television actor). In the face of a growing deterioration it was purchased in 1963 by Robert Madsen, who restored the exterior, refurbished the interior, and remodeled the adjacent carriage house. In my conversation with Robert Madsen, he recounted that his decision to use a striking Valentine color scheme prompted a friend to inquire teasingly if he meant to call his investment "Pink Lady or Pink Elephant." Since then it has been put to commercial use, claiming over the years a Pink Lady restaurant, an antique store, an architect's office, an interior decorating shop, and a realty firm. For vintage sake there are portraits of the senior William Carson and his son John Milton in the entry hall. And for his labors as he describes them in a brochure of his own (with a pinkish cover and a lovely drawing of the house), Robert Madsen was "the first recipient of the City of Eureka Certificate of Merit Award for the restoration and preservation of a Victorian home."

Exterior Highlights

The front elevation sketch of the Carson Mansion by the Newsoms, so frequently encountered in books on American architectural history, would appear to have been followed quite faithfully. While the original plan called for a "two-story and basement frame residence," a third story and a tower were incorporated. So the residence evolved as a structure of eighteen rooms. It is solidly built of Douglas fir, each wall outside and inside supported by separate foundations as a protection against winter gales, rains, and earthquakes. The porch, a spacious outdoor living room, is propped up by cyclopean pillars turned and ornamented. The veranda (balcony) on the second story is encircled by a wrought-iron framework, overlaid at the intervals just above the west and south entrances by the insignia of the Masonic Order (of which Carson was a member) interlaced with his initials W. C. The complex of windows at the different elevations (dormers and oriels) are enhanced by lacelike lattice. The profile bristles with gables, turrets, cupolas, and pillars, capped by massive mouldings which teem with the woodcarver's art. Under the gabled roof lines are bargeboards with their own figments of sawn idioms. The sloping roofs are crowned with finials, perhaps suggesting the underlying restlessness of the times or the aspiration to heaven. The lordly tower represents somewhat the offspring of a mansard roof with its slightly concave arc.

The exterior walls are finished in redwood, utilizing shingles adorned with a massive application of scrolls and curlicues. In perspective the profile is irregular, a fairyland of architectural wonderment. The chimneys are scarcely discernible, offering no intrusion to the eye sweeping in the broad outline. While the three gables in terraced ranking to the rear of the residence (eastward) present a rhythmic view from a distance, a close-up of the back entrance confirms that the Gothic Revival made no effort to establish architectural beauty in the more functional area. At night, however, the impact of the looming residence upon a viewer might be different, possibly an eerie feeling as the modest lighting effects play upon the exterior, especially on what seem like sinister-looking windows. The shadings of green seem to endow the ornamentation with a ghoulish meaning and together with the darkening contrast of the wooden landscape suggest a moment of suspense in a Gothic mystery novel.

An interesting conversational piece relates to the tower at the top with its steeply-sloped gabled roof and crowning ornamented finial. Oscar Lewis, a prolific writer on the West Coast past, in *Here Lived the Californians* (1957, p. 142), passes on a story, apparently handed down orally, that it was the custom of Carson to climb daily the balustered back stairway to the tower. From either the enclosed small room or the surrounding open balconies he could scan with powerful binoculars the horizon for glimpses of schooners approaching the bay after lengthy voyages. This custom would seem to have originated in New England where homes overlooking the Atlantic coast included towers girded by a fully-developed "captain's walk." Not infrequently, if the spouse outlived her mate, the proper reference would be the "widow's walk." In the Carson Mansion the tower and the open balconies suggest the bridge of a ship and to make the nautical imagery even more realistic there is the sawn idiom of life preservers suspended from the railings.

Bangs, in *Portals West* (1960, p. 20) draws a comparison in this respect between the Carson Mansion and that of Louis Portal, French immigrant and successful operator of laundries in San Francisco. The latter utilized the tower in his rural retreat of 400 acres at Cupertino in the Santa Clara valley to bring the toilers in the field below within the purview of a spyglass. No less effective, it has been said, was the tower to watch roving herds in lieu of riding the range constantly. Incidentally, Bangs notes that "it is interesting to observe the similarity in the dominant composition of this lavish residence [Carson Mansion] and of its prototype in the Portal House [p. 24 and plate 3]."

The reader should be aware that some alterations have been made over the years in the details of the exterior. The facts may be deduced by a comparison between a modern-day photograph of the Carson Mansion and one taken about 1890 to be found in the beautiful collection assembled in book form by Peter E. Palmquist, *Fine California Views: The Photographs of A. W. Ericson* (1975, p. 45). Originally the finials gracing the ridges of the sloping gables and the peaked tops of the corner round turrets were slender metallic spikes. For whatever reason—eroding or falling off—they are now turned wood ornamentals simply by the removal of the metallic tips. Similarly, the iron cresting which enclosed the balcony at the rear of the tower has been replaced by a wooden balustrade. The ridges of the sloping gables have been treated likewise, a wooden edging substituted for the serrated cresting. Nor are the exterior chimneys prominent, apparently removed because of unsteadiness, according to Baird's data book report on the Carson Mansion (1964), with local newspapers fixing the blame specifically on the earthquake of December 1954. Equally worth mention is the set of 28 black-and-white photographs assembled for the Historic American Buildings Survey, including profiles in 1902 and 1960, cross-section views of the exterior, and close-ups of the interior (mainly rooms and hallways on the first and second floors), plus the front elevation sketch by the architects.

Perhaps the most marked change visible to the naked eye is the absence of the once contrasting colors of black and white shingles on the gabled roofs, the eaves over the porch, and on the roof of the woodshed. The commentary attached to the above 1890 photograph suggests the combination might be shingles with the reddish tint of the redwood and tin flashings set off by exterior sidings yellowish with red trim. But a very close examination of an enlarged photograph on the wall of a room of the tenanted architects in the "Pink Lady" across the street suggests strongly that the presumed tin flashings were nothing more than shingles shaped in the form of fish scales and painted white, especially the tapering gable above the tower. Since then the roofs have been shingled in routine fashion and the exterior painted in contrasting grayish greens referred to by Eurekans as "cream and spinach."

Quite unique from an architectural point of view is the turret off the westerly corner fronting M Street and not easily discernible to the spectator. It is not brought down to the ground but rests on a bracket and technically shares the nomenclature of an oriel along with the bay window. No less intriguing is the speculation whether the Carson Mansion mirrors the character of the owner or must be viewed simply as an object of symmetry and impressiveness. As architectural historians exchange thoughts on psychological inferences attached to residences, the French Accent is dynamic, the Italianate exudes dignity, and the Gothic (presumably both Stick-Eastlake and Queen Anne) invokes an inspiring spirit. Indeed, it is argued that some types of homes encourage an orderly existence and others reflect a sense of freedom in one's life style. The direction which the Carson home took would seem to require a case history of the family individually and collectively.

CARSON MANSION: AN INTERPRETATION

A most fascinating aspect of the exterior is the use of wood motifs, often dubbed "gingerbread." The word referred to English cakes flavored with ginger and cut into fancy shapes. Subsequently the word was extended to the carved and gilded decorations sported by a sailing vessel, and finally to gaudy embellishments on home exteriors. Its widespread use in the less pretentious Victorian cottages has prompted some writers to describe "gingerbread" as folk art. As applied on the outside surfaces it is likened to a banner hung out for a celebration, symbolizing confidence in a land of opportunity and the importance attached to the individual person. In particular the sawn ornament represented an expression of the boldness and courage inherent in frontier settlements. From the porch apron to the roof finial the fanciful designs of flamboyant imaginations proclaimed a revivified nation on the march. For the discussion which follows on the many ways the scrolls and curlicues might be interpreted meaningfully, the book by Ben Karp, *Wood Motifs in American Domestic Architecture* (1966) merits examination.

The challenge is to classify the vocabulary of "gingerbread" adorning the Eurekan showplace. Its sawn idioms run the gamut of the language of ceremonial hieratics—abstractions, mysteries, functionals. Only modestly would the calligraphy of *holes, slits,* and *slots* seem to be utilized. They are space and not substance and are sawn in the woodboards such as aprons, brackets, and bargeboards. A slot is a wider slit and may take various shapes—round, square, leaf, diamond, club, heart. Most readily identifiable in the Carson Mansion are the open eyes of the porch apron peeking through the shrubs and bushes encircling the base of the house. The *stick dance* is used as decorations under roofs and as porch railings. They consist of the odds and ends of lumber strewn around the carpenter's workshop. They are free from the constraints of being verticals and horizontals, appearing rather at intervals in rhythmic variety and as spatial transpositions. They can be nailed together in any openings as intersecting sticks attuned to a rich orchestration of themes. Perhaps the best examples of the stick dance on the exterior of the Carson Mansion, and by no means easy to spot, may be seen under the gables and about the balconies.

More obvious is the shingle idiom for the exterior surface of the Carson Mansion, an easier means to sheath a house than sawn clapboard siding. What made it possible was the bandsaw which could turn out any desired shape with ease and speed. The full repertory could include shapes suggesting fruits, garden produce, playing cards, and flowers. The most common variety is the cut round shingle derived from fish scales, which when exposed looks like plumage. Hence the terminology of the wood motifs as *scales* and *feathers.* In varied strokes the shingles establish clearly defined areas and their projections provide a relationship with the adjacent parts of the structure. Equally predominant in the Carson Mansion are the attached *appliqués*, nailed on bargeboards, dormer windows, brackets, and eaves. They are of every imaginable design and float as it were against the surface in non-contiguous units. A greater delicacy is attainable since such ornamentation does not structurally require viable contact for support. The bracket, often regarded as the oratory of the carpentry, looms as articulated wood with capricious notions for varying its path from the post to the lintel. The total result is a sense of exuberance and color wedded in a dazzling display.

Karp makes much of the wood motif as a purveyor of imagery. If it is not always easy to decipher a given sawn ornamentation, the effort to perceive the Carson Mansion in flights of fancy can bring its rewards in cultural enlivenment. For one thing, the game may be played to identify the mime in the abstractions. The bedecked brackets on the porch might be construed as welcoming gestures or playful greetings. The *appliqués* may imply sculpture in the round, ready to spring, to leap, to whirl their way into the open. Or in such guises as floral designs and the sun's rays the inference could be preparations for a festive gathering. For a second thing, the game may be played to identify the wood motif in the fugitive world of light and shadow. Sawn idioms can import a luminosity to surfaces, dispersing the fragmentations of spotted light much in the fashion of impressionist technique in painting. The shifting illumination of the surface as the sun moves across the sky beset often by a cover of clouds at varying angles can take all manner of silhouettes. Scalloped fish scales may dot the exterior wall with foliage or sparkling waters. Brackets may radiate striking lines as they come forth in the failing light of early evening. For a third thing, the game may be played to identify wood motifs as representations of earthly objects. The combinations of tortured sticks beneath the gabled towers may be conceived as snow icicles slowly dripping downwards. The turned columns on the porch may offer the illusion of table legs and billiard balls. The ellipticals under the porch eaves have the appearance of an abacus. Yet, if the effect is a world of picturesqueness, some degree of stateliness and dignity could be equally claimed in the totality.

To conclude the discussion of the exterior of the Carson Mansion, if the following summations by architectural historians may infer that the last word has not yet been spoken or written, they do comprise an interesting set of observations. The Federal Writers' Project, *California: A Guide to the Golden State* (1954, p. 354) comments that "the tortured ornamentation and the trim paint give it the air of a prop for a Silly Symphony." A more restrained comment is carried in its edition of 1967 (p. 354) to the effect that "the Carson Mansion . . . is an example of flamboyant Victorian architecture, the peak of the woodworkers' art." Perusse in his article on the Gothic

Revival in California (1955) speaks of the "capricious Carson House." An unsigned article in the *Michigan Society of Architects, Monthly Bulletin* (May 1959, pp. 12-13) describes it as "built during the time of the moguls [and] it is the Kohinoor of the gingerbread age." Wayne Andrews, Archives of American Art Professor at Wayne State University, in *House Beautiful* (February 1965), albeit marred by a misspelling of the Newsoms' name and an error in the date of construction, notes that "this monument to the ambition of a local lumber baron may not be a work of art [;] but few works of art are as unforgettable as this businessman's bid for immortality."

Davidson in *The American Heritage of Antiques* (1969, p. 312) refers to the profile as a "what-not," possessing "a basic construction concealed by or overlaid with a mixed confection of motifs borrowed from everywhere and nowhere." Indeed, he includes the front elevation sketch in a section of *The American Heritage History of Notable Houses* (1971, p. 261) entitled, "Architectural Follies: Styles Unlimited." Maass in *The Victorian Home in America* (1972, p. 166) quotes an unnamed historian (who can be identified as Baird, in the data book report of 1964) as characterizing it "so aggressively frightful as to be enchanting." Most recently, Wrenn and Mulloy in *America's Forgotten Architecture* (1976, p. 72) averred that the Carson Mansion "built as a testimonial to the possibilities of wood in 1889 [correctly, 1884-85] . . . epitomizes Victorian elegance with a paint scheme outlining its obvious charms."

For a vignette in a lighter vein to the riddle of architectural style, one may turn to the *California Architect and Building News* (November 1884, p. 205) during the heyday of the Gothic Revival. The news item is captioned "Queen Anne Hodge-Podge" and goes as follows:

> "Architect - Well I declare that is a pretty fair house plan for an amateur, only you have left no space for stairways and closets. Did you make it yourself?
> Prospective Builder - Yes, but the only thing that puzzles me is to know what style of cottage it is. It is not Gothic, nor Italian, nor—
> Architect - No, it is absolutely nothing. As to style, it is simply a meaningless hodge-podge, to be frank with you.
> Prospective Builder - Well, what shall I call it, have you no name for hodge-podges?
> Architect - Oh! yes. We call 'em Queen Annes."

In any instance, the counsel to a bewildered public might be to approach the exterior of the Carson Mansion as a human story unfolding in distinct chapters the quest for a reconciliation between man and nature.

Side entrance, from *Historic American Buildings Survey*, 1960.

Close-up of cyclopean pillars
of the principal porch
which encircles the west and south
sides of the house.

Southwest corner, from *Historic American Buildings Survey,* 1960.

Tower and south gable,
from *Historic American Buildings
Survey*, 1960.

West gable, from *Historic
American Buildings Survey*,
1960.

Profile of tower from the west, from *Historic American Buildings Survey*, 1960.

Tower room and balcony and skylight over ballroom, from *Historic American Buildings Survey*, 1960.

CHAPTER FOUR

CARSON MANSION: A NARRATIVE

Newsom Brothers, Architects

LET US TURN OUR ATTENTION NOW to the interior of the Carson Mansion. It is said that the Gothic Revival home was planned from the inside out and that the layout of the interior had something to do with the outward look. An assurance of sunlight or shade in rooms at certain times of the day could dictate the irregularities of the exterior. A pertinent observation in this respect is to be found in Bangs, *Portals West* (1960, p. 13):

> "The American Gothic broke free of tradition and permitted planning from the inside out and let the grouping of rooms, arranged for function, determine the exterior aspect of the structure. Wings could be sent out in any direction and these in turn, when collected by porches and verandas, achieved the desired unity.... Its advent marked a departure from the old concept of planning and it was to see more innovations and the development of more domestic amenities than had occurred in any similar period."

On the supposition that Carson followed the advice of his architects in matters related to the interior as well as to the exterior, the views of the Newsoms merit consideration. In their four volumes they set down a number of specific requirements for a pretentious home. As a start they would stress a central hall, innovative sliding doors on the first floor for flexibility of party space, parquet floors, high ceilings, luxurious fireplaces, and open stairways with ramped rails and twisting balusters. For everyday use by family and servants there should be a second stairway of simple style at the rear. Parlors and drawing rooms should be large and whenever possible include cozy nooks and arched recesses. The kitchen ought to be of ample space and contain the latest facilities in the way of cooking ranges, hot and cold running water, and central heating. Both gas and electrical equipment, supplementing each other, were very desirable. Bathrooms needed to be generous in size and to include tubs, indoor toilets, and modern plumbing. Bedrooms were best situated over the parlors and drawing rooms and the bathrooms over the kitchen. The dining room should be planned to accentuate opportunities for parties and to show off the sideboard (buffet) with its china service. As for storage space the possibilities were available in provisions for a basement and an attic.

Not a few of the desirable features listed by the Newsoms come close to those to be encountered in the Carson Mansion. Both a vestibule and a front entry should be included, the latter enhanced by double doors with cathedral-type stained glass panels. A grand hall lent dignity and allowed the spirit to grow whereas a narrow space nurtured a dull mind. The open staircase could have seats and spindle fillings for the space about the rails. For parlor and drawing room they favored onyx fireplaces and mantels with tiled hearths in preference to redwood and hardwood. For the dining room they favored a paneled wall and a sideboard fitted out attractively with drawers, shelves, lockers, and glass doors. The library might be papered or tinted and furnished with glass bookcases. The tropical hardwoods of Central America and the California redwoods were recommended as the most suitable woods, the selection to be gay for the drawing room, somber for the library, comfortable for the dining room, elegant for the boudoir, and cozy for the smoking and billiard rooms. If they regarded mahogany as the most beautiful wood known to mankind, its heaviness could be compensated for by a blend with a lighter wood. For decorative tone, especially in the bathroom and the vestibule, glazed and enameled tile merited consideration.

No less decisive were the Newsoms on the intimate details of interior furnishings. The quotation is to be found in Baird's book (1964) and would seem to be a composite of extracts from the Newsoms' volumes on house plans for "cheerful homes in the free style of architecture." Again, there is much akin to what may be seen in the Carson Mansion:

"Almost all have modern improvements such as electric Bells, electric Lighters for the gas Fixtures, hardwood Mantels, Art Tiles, Bronze Hardware, open work plumbing, tiled Vestibule, Spindle Arches, swell Shelves, and a tasty Staircase lighted with domed Skylight. These residences are generally finished interiorly with fine hardwoods and Redwood, interspersed with Dados of Lincrusta-Walton [a trademark applied to a variety of fabric made of canvas and treated with layers of thickened linseed oil, stamped with decorative patterns, and used for ceiling and wall hangings—some 100 designs were available in combination with wall paper or any other flat decoration]. The Art Glass is very rich Bevel Plate with copper Bars. By throwing back the Sliding-doors, the Lower Floor of such a house can be made into one large room—admirably suited for Receptions. Off the Dining-room there is often a Recessed Fire-place and Smokery or lounging Den. The kitchen is well ventilated and has its Store closet, Butlers' closet and Pass to the Dining-room. On the Upper floor there are large Chambers, well lighted with Bays. Throughout, the Interior is full of novel features, and well planned for Furniture."

For the rest, the Newsoms had equally positive views on the decoration of the interior walls:

"White walls unrelieved by any color are relics of barbarism, and are almost a thing of the past . . . and a house is incomplete without adornments. In reception rooms and drawing rooms light, cheerful effects are sought after. In dens, dining rooms, and halls, rich, dark, and medium colors are best suited. In the library and chambers, according to the situation and capacity, for light medium colors, blue, pink, and such shades as harmonize with surroundings are most suitable. . . . As papers are now designed and finished it is no difficult matter for those with limited purses to accomplish [it]. . . . A visit to any leading and responsible Paper House will convince one of this, and may result in making cozy, comfortable and pleasing to the eye what otherwise might be a plain monotony, cold and unendurable."

Interior Highlights

That the interior of the Carson Mansion measured up to the exacting standards of the Newsoms is the subject of the next several pages. And Kirker would note "the increasing number of Neo-Victorians who find in its spacious rooms, mahogany-panelled nooks, and great halls an escape from the cramped, unimaginative, and bleak dimensions of contemporary housing."

A considerable amount of building materials were brought in from other parts of the world. Of course he used choice clear-grain redwoods, carefully prepared in his own mills for much of the interior paneling. But, as Bangs observes in *Portals West* (1960, p. 24), even though Carson's fortune was made from the redwood, the lumber magnate manifested an unprejudiced taste for other kinds of woods. He dispatched a schooner to bring back from Central America some 97,000 feet of primavera, a beautiful light-toned hardwood often called white mahogany. Similarly, he imported complements of mahogany from the Philippines and teakwood from East India. For his fireplaces he sought out the onyx quarries in

Mexico, so highly favored by the Newsoms. No doubt, too, San Francisco was a source for many items unobtainable locally and the Newsom booklets with their array of advertisements of the latest in building supplies could well have been poured over for hours by the Carson household.

Several sources are available for descriptions of the interior. The celebration of the golden anniversary of the marriage of John Milton and his wife was featured in the local newspapers (September 29-30, October 1, 1937) by a description of their home. Both pictures and commentaries may be found in the *Times* (March 12, 1950) and the *Standard* (March 13, 1950) on the occasion of the sale of the Carson Mansion to a private social club. An article in the *Times* (March 5, 1967) contains not only a description but several excellent photographs. The Ingomar Club itself issued (*circa* 1970) an eight-page guide, presenting color photos of several rooms along with commentaries. The previously referred-to account by Beal, *Carson's Red Castle* (1973) has unusually regal scenes of some of the rooms along with commentaries. A number of books by architectural historians provide one or two shots, most often of the front entry and the staircase. The writer expresses his own deep appreciation for an opportunity to tour the interior and to see firsthand how the realities compare with the information gathered from the above sources.

The front passage is through storm doors and a small vestibule, a necessary intermediary between the elements of the weather and security for the massive double doors which constitute the formal entrance into the Carson Mansion. Each door possesses a stained glass panel with life-sized figures said to have been copied from Shakespearean plays. The male is fully armored for battle and the female could well be taking a stroll with her dog as companion. Above the double doors is a transom which likewise contains a stained glass panel, depicting a male in somber thought, with an intricate design as the border. Flanking an outer hallway as it were are two arched recesses done in primavera and bedecked with relief carvings. A statue of a flower boy and a bench seat also in primavera are off to the side along a corridor leading to the back rooms. The main hallway may be described as offering the viewer a sensation of soaring upwards. The grand stairway is constructed also of primavera, the light color of which creates an airy and fanciful effect. Most compelling, as one mounts the stairway, is an immense encased stained glass window. It is divided into four panels by carved wood frames, each bearing a life-sized figure clad in the rich costumes of the middle ages and engaged in his or her artistic occupation. From left to right, as one ascends the stairs, the three vertical panels represent the arts of painting, drama, and general science while the horizontal panel above depicts a musician and his instruments. The brilliant shadings in the bits of colored glass are said to present a startling effect in the afternoon as the sun streams through the vividly-embossed windows.

To the left of the hallway as one enters is the drawing room, often referred to as the music room. The onyx fireplace is flanked by a mantel of redwood panels while the mantel itself is superbly-carved Philippine mahogany in leaf design. Merrill Folsom, a free-lance writer, in *More Great American Mansions and Their Stories* (1967, p. 167), notes that "this fireplace has a double flue which divides so that a lead glass window is above... where a solid chimney ordinarily would be." The lead glass window is a stained glass panel revealing a lady in a flowing gown with the borders in geometric designs. A window alcove is framed in all three types of redwood grain, burl, curly, and clear. Both the drapes and the plush upholstered chairs are a deep red and are said to be part of the original furnishings. Where the organ, custom-made for the room, used to repose, is now a pedal-operated organ contributed by one of the members of the social club which owns the property. At the top of each window peering forth through the inner lacy curtains are small stained glass panels, the circular part featuring bird and foliage and the squared border colored stones in geometric design. Mention might also be made of a secretary desk in one corner and a gilted-marble decorative stand with a sculpture of the upper body and head of a woman. The wall covering is a lovely floriated brocade cloth and the ceiling is vaulted. An interesting riddle is an oil portrait of a young girl, perhaps their daughter Lottie Carson, for it matches her photograph taken with a brother at a childhood age (*Fountain Papers*, vol. 2, p. 00006).

To the right of the hallway is the main living room or parlor where three generations of Carsons received guests and held formal receptions. The central motif is a fireplace with an ornate onyx base and mantel surmounted by a large mirror encased in a carved gilt frame reaching almost to the ceiling. In its glow and mottled depth the majestic onyx reflects the loveliest crystal. As Folsom (1967, p. 167) recalls his impression, "the onyx is pinkish, partly translucent and with a quartz-like effect sometimes seen in a fine rose crystal." More than this, the beautiful mirror has a way of reflecting the dignity of the alabaster chandelier in the center of the room. There are comfortable sofas and chairs and a small table with curved and clawed legs suggestive of the decorative furniture of eighteenth-century European palaces. The several lengthy windows are enhanced by long flowing brownish velvet drapes. Here too at the top of each window, but scarcely discernible through the inner lacy curtains are small stained glass panels, featuring in the center representations of bird or foliage and bordered by colored stones in geometric design. An equally interesting riddle is an oil portrait of a young boy, perhaps that of John Milton.

The dining room is referred to in all accounts as "baronial," featuring an elegant and long oaken dining table capable of seating twenty-six people according to the literature. But there are only a dozen upright chairs upholstered with French tapestry. An immense and glistening oaken sideboard stands against the wall and may well have been specially built to match the other furniture in the room. The sideboard possesses open shelves, built-in glass cupboards, beveled mirrors (said to have been imported from England's finest glass houses), and ample drawer space. As in other rooms there is an alabaster chandelier centered over the dining table. The fireplace has a carved oak frame and above the mantel piece is a beveled mirror. Candelabras repose on the mantel shelf with bric-a-brac in the two niches on each side of the mirror. There is a small server with mirror, perhaps part of the old furnishings. The lower part of the walls is wainscoted with the rest matted to the ceiling. Rather startling is a second dining table, round in shape, large enough for seating several people, and located next to a bay window looking out upon the landscape. Perhaps its informality was preferred for everyday meals to the more august setting. The formal entry is from the hallway and the collected drapes at each side along with the carved posts must have been an impressive sight in the glow of evening festivities.

A familiar story in the literature is attributed to Clarence La Boyteaux, husband of third-generation Bell Carson (the daughter of John Milton). He is quoted as saying that while on a visit to the Chapultepec Castle in Mexico City he saw there a dining room which was an exact counterpart, even to the hardware on the inner doors. William Carson is mentioned as having taken trips to Mexico on business and possibly had admired its beauty. Or perhaps the inspiration came from the Newsoms who, touring Mexico themselves, saw in the dining room a design worthy of repeating for an affluent client. Curiosity prompted a letter to the National Museum of History in Mexico City and in due time a photograph of the dining room in Chapultepec Castle was forwarded. There would seem to be a considerable likeness in several features. An oblong table and a dozen upright chairs elaborately upholstered are strong reminders. There is a similarly-positioned fireplace, albeit encasing above the mantel a large painting rather than a mirror. Instead of ornately-leafed wooden frames, however, there are at each side of the mantel the carved naked torso and head of a young lady with arms extended overhead. While the details are not too clear in the photograph, one can discern a similarly-positioned sideboard and draped entry. In his data book report (1964) Baird agreed, whatever might be the sources he used for comparison, that there were some similarities in shape and general character although the dining room in Chapultepec Castle "is much larger in scale ... and the wood dadoes, overmantels and cupboards differ in details." It might be added that the ill-fated Austrian Archduke Ferdinand Maximilian, emperor of Mexico from 1864 to 1867, and his wife the Empress Carlotta converted Chapultepec Castle during their brief reign into a luxurious palace and no doubt the dining room was included in the renovations.

Opposite the dining room, down the hallway and near the back stairway, there is a small paneled den, presumably an office and retreat for the man of the family. There is a fireplace, making four in all downstairs. A rolltop desk reposes in a corner. Along one wall there is a built-in glass case, its shelves displaying a number of stuffed game birds, perhaps in keeping with the sporting proclivities attached to the masculine. Increasing further the crowded appearance of the den is an open cage elevette, apparently a late addition by John Milton's wife, for her husband died in August 1941 while her death was not until January 1944. Such would seem to be the fact if a letter now adorning the den wall as an amusing relic of the past is accurate. It is from a maintenance company (dated October 27, 1975) informing John Milton that its records showed no repairs since the installation some thirty-four years ago and perhaps a "fresh look" should now be given the elevette. The open space cut into the ceiling for ascent to the second floor has now been sealed. For the rest, it should be noted that there is a small room off the pantry where the Carson generations had their breakfast. And throughout the first floor, in keeping with the preference of the Newsoms, sliding doors offer flexibility for privacy or additional entertainment space.

Upstairs an elegant and formal hallway is the distinguishing feature. The series of rounded archways show an Oriental or Moorish influence. They are done in plaster and stained to resemble wood and are heavy with carving and fretwork. Some of the molds are reported to be still in the basement. By the top of the staircase sealing off the hallway from the stairwell are a pair of richly-polished burl redwood pillars, presenting a striking contrast to the light-toned primavera base and railings. The posts are robustly turned to reflect both the dignity and the luxury of the interior. At the end of the hallway the gaze meets three lovely stained glass panels in a modernistic style of configurations regarded as unusual for the eighteen-eighties. Above these stained glass panels there is still another one, the familiar small panel with the light oval part displaying its bird or foliage and bordered by the usual geometric design. Incidentally, these stained glass panels are being redone now, for they are showing signs of wear and buckling. Darkish velvety drapes flow on each side, tastefully setting off a piano (contributed by a member of the social club), the piano stool, and two sofa armchairs. The imposing hallway must have been a temptation to the children whose natural tendency would have been to romp and to slide down banisters.

The principle room on the second floor is another parlor, also boasting an onyx fireplace with a large mirror bordered in a gilt frame similar to the one downstairs. The presence of a glassed bookcase and old editions which one might call furniture pieces suggested that the parlor also served as a library. Besides the ninth edition of the *Encyclopaedia Britannica* and a collection of literary classics, the varied holdings reflect some leaning towards American history. A wide expanse of windows lend an airiness for intimate gatherings of the clan. During the daytime the fine lacework curtains filter through the sunlight and soften its brightness while the heavy drapes assure a secure privacy in the evening.

The remainder of the second floor was given over to bedrooms. There were four bedrooms, two of which were connected with one bathroom. The other two may be described as having been bedroom suites. While none of the bedroom pieces now remain, it is said that spacious wardrobe chests were designed to match the fittings. The bathrooms are good-sized and look very simple and plain now with their white walls and white porcelain tubs, washstands, and toilets. There are three fireplaces on the second floor. Special treatment is accorded some of the windows, framed in arches and bow-shaped and rimmed with carved embellishments. And as usual above the windows are the dainty stained glass panels with their oval scene of nature and border of geometric design.

Once again it might be of interest to include some observations of Baird in his data book report (1964), this time of the interior:

> " . . . The mansion contained eighteen rooms. . . . A squared vestibule with double doors (the outer door is a sliding one; the inner doors are a pair of tall wood doors with stained glass windows and stained glass transom above). . . . The parlors have Mexican onyx mantels and either a carved mahogany and redwood overmantel with stained glass window (left parlor) or large mirror (right parlor). Parlor walls are either painted or fabric covered, and do not presently reflect the original wall coverings [perhaps Lincrusta-Walton]. Ceilings throughout the first floor have raised plaster geometric patterns, vaguely suggestive of the ceilings of the sixteenth century. At the cornice level are elaborate carved wood bracketed cornices, or less elaborate plaster cornices. Here the approach of more 'correct' Period ornament can be seen in rows of egg and dart or other modified Classical moldings. The wood work, particularly in the vestibule and entrance stair hall, on the other hand, reflects the bizarre local variations on Eastlake, Tudor and Mannerist sources. Plaster rosettes in the center of the principal rooms' ceilings once focussed attention on gasoliers; the present fixtures are electric and date from the twenties and fifties of the twentieth century. . . . There is a large drawing room on the second floor—also with an onyx mantel, surmounted by a massive mirror. Perhaps the strangest single feature of the second floor

is the hallway with its horse shoe arches of carved wood [*sic* - plaster]—now painted. Cornice details on this floor, as on the first, reflect more 'correct' Period styling—have Classical moldings.... Doors and door frames are similar on both first and second floors; pseudo-fluted pilasters of an entirely 'original' design frame doors with three vertical recessed panels over four rectilineer recessed panels. Continuing the frame over the door are grouped moldings approaching Classical types. Hardware is generally original; lighting fixtures on the second floor are modern...."

The third floor has its special features. Most prominent is a ballroom whose expanse for dancing was ample perhaps for as many as ten couples. Around its walls were said to have been paintings, etchings, and steel engravings, many purchased at Gump's of San Francisco, well-known dealer in fine decorative pieces. Perhaps this was accomplished during August 1885 when William Carson and his wife spent two weeks in the Golden City. Then there was a billiard room nearby replete with racks of cues attached on the wall ready for those prepared to try their skill. Both may be regarded as progenitors of the modern-day recreation room or den in the basement. Certainly, in those days, the well-to-do families preferred providing such facilities at home to having children patronize the suspect pool parlors and dancing halls in the downtown district. In addition, there were three bedrooms sharing one bath and no fireplaces. Presumably they were used by servants and reached by the back stairway. This same stairway leads up to the observation tower, conceivably a fourth floor for the small room gathered inside. It would not seem too far-fetched to suggest that the attributes of the third floor reflected the Victorian tradition among upper class society to locate apart the children and the servants from their own daily lives.

Besides some of the original furnishings which may still be seen in the Carson Mansion and those listed from descriptive accounts, a catalogue of memorabilia merits mention. The handsome grandfather's clock imported from England a century ago stands in the main hallway and is as accurate as ever. At the side of each onyx fireplace is a brass andiron and a finely-wrought Japanese container as a coal base. In the music room are two treasured antique hangings in the form of gold and brown panels that were reputed to have once graced the walls of a Chinese temple in Peiping (possibly an acquisition of John Milton and his wife while touring the Far East). On a shelf next to the glassed bookcase in the parlor on the second floor is an old family Bible enshrined in a protective glass case. On the third story at the head of the back stairs leading to the tower there rests on the floor an initialled "WC" weather-beaten sea chest with the label of the famed Hotel del Coronado (a Gothic Revival of Queen Anne style in its own right) pasted on the outside. In the same back stairway area there is mounted on the wall with a slab of redwood burl the head and antlers of an elk, a sort of sentinel guarding the entrance to the lofty tower room and no doubt a hunting trophy of the Carson clan. While the music room now possesses wallpaper, it might well be a replacement for the Lincrusta-Walton fabrics so highly recommended by the Newsoms to clients (and inferred by the foregoing lengthy quotation by Baird).

For the rest, the general complement of Victorian furnishings as described by Meyric Rogers, an art authority on furniture and a past museum curator at Yale University, in *American Interior Designs* (1947) might fill in the glaring gaps. If the impression is one of crammed surroundings, the intent was solid comfort. Beyond the staple articles established by long usage, a multitude of secondary objects occupied any vacant space not necessary for family circulation. In the hallway side tables and chairs were supplemented with umbrella stands, hatracks, coat hangers, and mirrors. Furthermore, an inglenook (chimney corner) and a fireplace might offer symbols of hospitality for the arriving guest. In the parlor and drawing room the furnishings would include tufted ottomans, overstuffed chairs, easy chairs with fringed cushions and buttoned upholstery protected by antimacassars, patented rockers, and a sprinkling of gilded and beribboned chairs. Equally obvious would be a variety of small marble-topped tables and stands covered with heavy-fringed velours.

Navigation in this "sea of plenty" could be hazardous since most tables bore an ample quota of ornaments, souvenir knicknacks, and lamps "to trap the unwary." The lower parts of the walls were probably occupied by "whatnots and cabinets" while the upper reaches might be clad in flock paper of florid pattern or somber tone and lavishly bedecked with oil portraits and watercolor landscapes, all encased in depths of involved gilding. The dining room had its carved and lumpy glory, assembling a fashioned sideboard for bone and porcelain ware and settings, a dining table round or square, small serving tables, and a few but striking canvasses on the walls. The library or study would be lined with glassed-in bookcases having leather-valanced shelves or cabinets and the wall space crowded with engravings and sporting prints. For masculine comfort there would be massive leather chairs and to handle household bookkeeping chores a roll-top desk. The predominant furniture piece in a bedroom would be a massive walnut bed with head draperies, later replaced by knobbed brass with swinging wings flanking the head of the bed. Other staple articles could comprise dressing tables, lounge chairs, and a bureau or two. For the windows the details might tabulate blinds, shutters, muslin curtains, heavy velvet drapes, and tasseled variances.

Entry hall, from *Historic American Buildings Survey*, 1960.

Ceiling in stairway hall, from *Historic American Buildings Survey*, 1960.

Stained glass panels in entry hall double doors.

First floor stairway, from *Historic American Buildings Survey*, 1960.

Close-up of fireplace
and stained glass panel in
first floor drawing room.

First floor drawing room, also called music room,
from *Historic American Buildings Survey*, 1960.

First floor living room, from *Historic American Buildings Survey*, 1960.

Two views of dining room.

Stairway in second floor hall, showing Ingomar Plaque, from *Historic American Buildings Survey*, 1960.

Second floor hallway, from *Historic American Buildings Survey*, 1960.

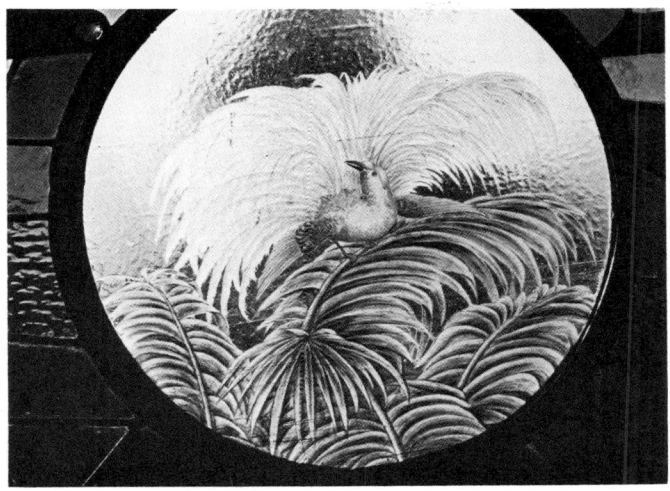

Typical stained glass panel showing bird and foliage.

Second floor living room, from *Historic American Buildings Survey*, 1960.

Third floor ballroom, now used for recreation room; shows some of carved plaques of Dr. Burre.

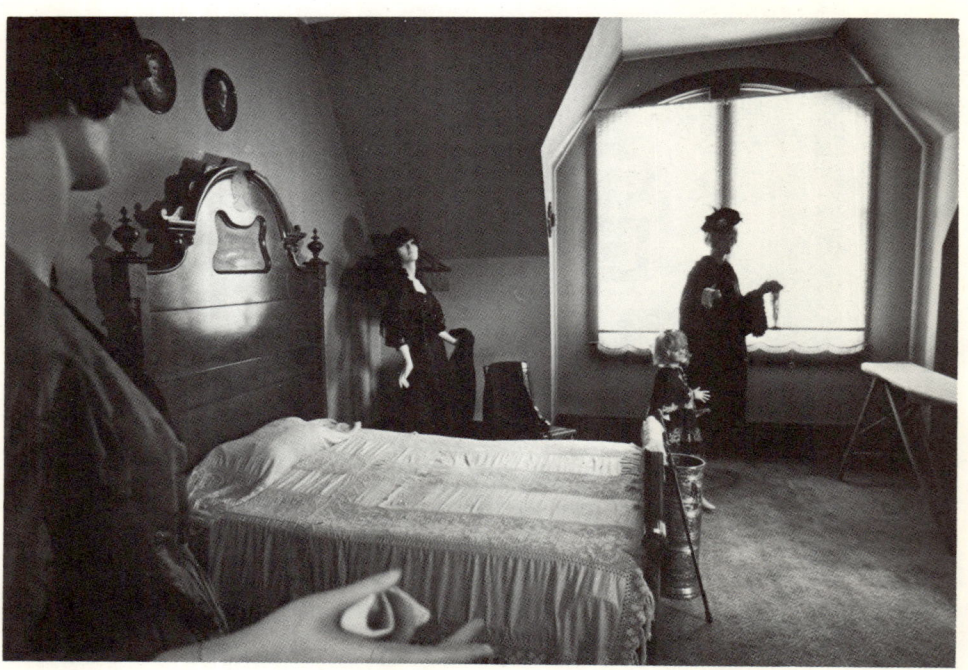

Third floor Historic Room.

Construction

Let us now pursue in narrative form this first venture of Carson in what might be called acculturation. The *Weekly Humboldt Times* (April 11, 1863) contains a reference to what was probably the earliest Carson residence and located in Bucksport to the south. A corroborative handwritten reference is included by Susie Baker Fountain, wife of a neighboring Blue Lake dentist and active in county historical research, in her *Papers* (vol. 2, p. 00015) to the effect that Carson bought some lots in 1862 in Bucksport. Presumably its construction must have been in anticipation of his marriage the following year to Sarah Wilson. The item in the local news column described the house going up as "a fine residence." After some ten years the Carsons moved to a residence located on the bluff overlooking the Bay Mill, part of the site later selected for the Carson Mansion. The *Fountain Papers* (vol. 2, p. 00014), dated January 31, 1872, contain some handwritten reminiscences which proffer the information that Carson "purchased a handsome new residence on the bluff lately erected by Dan Pickard [a bookkeeper at the Dolbeer and Carson mill] but vacated on the death of his wife." With the construction of the Carson Mansion the previous home was moved from its site to P Street with the front facing on Third Street. It is a good sized two-story house surrounded by rooming houses, duplexes, and single family houses, all wooden structures. Today it is still occupied although no doubt renovated from time to time. The exterior is blue with white trimming. The tall angular windows have pediments and very small brackets, perhaps suggestive of the Italianate. The roof is sloping, the apron face is plain, and the porch has a side entrance.

What might have been the thinking of Carson in deciding upon a new residence? There was the need for a larger home to accommodate his growing family. Perhaps he nurtured the hope that the edifice might represent the grandeur of the redwood country. Assuredly it must be a credit to the city where he lived and which he had helped to build. Indeed, even the thought could have been cherished that the enhanced standard of comfort, convenience, and aesthetic delight would be emulated by other citizens. Nor should the possibility be discounted that the lumber magnate may have wanted to demonstrate the wonderful things that could be done with the majestic redwood. That Carson was mindful of public opinion may be deduced from words attributed to him with regard to his proposed mansion. In the *Fountain Papers* (vol. 64, p. 262) there is an undated and unidentified newspaper clipping in which he is quoted as observing in a *pontifical voice* that "if I build poorly, they'll say I am a damn miser; if I build expensively they say I'm just trying to show off; so, I guess I'll build it to suit myself." In this connection, a conversation with an old-timer produced the story that

Carson waited until other wealthy citizens such as David Evans, Hans Henry Buhne, and John Vance (all lumbermen) had erected their residences in order to make his the most imposing. Perhaps this anecdote may be the basis for the contention of Folsom (1967, p. 166) that as the most prominent citizen Carson felt the need to outdo all others. In defense of Carson, if he had chosen to live in San Francisco instead of directing the mills on the scene and spending his money in Eureka, he could have been fancy free in the ostentatiousness of his home.

In any event, Carson would have derived great satisfaction from the appraisal by Leigh Hadley Irvine, one-time editor of the *Times*, in the *History of Humboldt County* (1915, pp. 609-610) that "the lovely residence was one of his most important contributions to the beautifying of his chosen city [and] the scene of the interests closest to his heart." And to the residents of Eureka today the mansion remains the symbol of a past concern for being in the mainstream of cultural developments. To carry further the subject of motivation and emulation, Gebhard and his co-authors in *A Guide to Architecture in San Francisco and Northern California* (1973, pp. 318-319) count over 75 well-preserved Victorian houses and buildings and include street maps showing the specific locations of some 50 of them. Their laudatory sentiments are capped with the observation that "if any community has the potential of being developed as the West Coast Williamsburg, it is Eureka." To which Professor William H. Pierson, Jr., emeritus professor of art at Williams College in Massachusetts, in an interview apropos his visit studying architecture on the Pacific coast (*Times-Standard*, May 12, 1974), would add that Eureka is real, . . . a celebration of abundance [whereas] Williamsburg is a museum piece, a make-believe, restored as it was supposed to be." By way of a postscript, in his own time Carson could at least take pride that the numerous Gothic Revival homes and buildings going up, however modest, were signs of a cultural consciousness. So does the Eureka chamber of commerce, announcing in one of its more recent brochures the availability of a map for a "Victorian Home Drive Tour."

For that matter, the editor of the *Times-Telephone* (July 29, 1884), as the *Times* was temporarily called from 1883-1886, showed awareness of this trend. His leader is captioned "The Era of Fine Dwellings" and is worth verbatim treatment:

> "In the building of fine cities there comes at some period of progress the era of fine buildings. Citizens seem to discard all at once their old surroundings and to put on the airs and graces of aesthetic taste. Whenever this awakening is felt in the matter of architecture the result is soon observed in the greatly increased beauty and costliness of dwellings. Men born with the love of beauty in their souls desire to

make the home beautiful above all things, and as wealth accumulates in a community this desire is given expression in the form of elegant houses and lovely grounds, particularly where there is abundant enterprise to back it.

The era of fine dwellings has reached Eureka or more strictly speaking, Eureka has reached that point in her progress best calculated to develop the latent aesthetic sense in the minds of her citizens. Old-fashioned, irregular, squatty and in every way ugly styles of architecture are giving place to neat and pretty cottage styles, and to something really magnificent in the style of more pretentious structures. The new cottages are too numerous to mention in detail. Of the pretentious and costly residences there are those erected and in course of erection by Messrs. Evans, Buhne, and Carson, which will do as fair examples of the style of modern architecture destined to be in vogue here in the future. The fact is our people have taste and artistic desires, hidden long in the dusty corners of the mind, it may be; but nevertheless coming to light under the generous auspices of prosperous times."

The earliest indication of what Carson had in mind I found in the *Times-Telephone* (August 29, 1883). In a column entitled "Bay City Jottings," frequently featured by the local newspaper, a correspondent in San Francisco reported in a letter dated August 26, 1883 that "William Carson will put up a fine dwelling house on his property; the [Richard] Sweasey and [Annie M.] Wilson lots [apparently in-laws by marriage]. The plans are all drawn up and work will probably commence soon." Subsequently, in the issue of September 11, 1883, the *Times-Telephone* inserted another letter from its San Francisco correspondent, dated September 8, which contained the information that "William Carson and his wife are in the city visiting at John Dolbeer's. Mr. Carson has some business to transact." A fair surmise would be that his business included consultation along with Sarah Wilson Carson with various architects in San Francisco. Perhaps the selection of the Newsoms as the architects was confirmed then.

The initial step in the actual construction could well have been the comment in the *Times-Telephone* (May 6, 1884) that "Carson and his wife have sailed for San Francisco on the *City of Chester* [May 3]." A fair surmise would be that the business at hand was to discuss final details with the Newsoms. Subsequently, on June 26, the *Standard* noted the arrival of Joseph Cather Newsom from San Francisco on the *City of Chester*. A week later, on July 1, the *Times-Telephone* announced in its columns that Samuel and Joseph Cather Newsom, architects with their principal office in San Francisco, had opened a branch in Eureka, at the headquarters of the Dolbeer and Carson Lumber Company (practically across the street from the building site). This was supplemented on the next page by an advertisement: "Architects and Superintendents of Construction; Eastlake Style a

Specialty." That the Newsoms lost little time in capitalizing on their engagement by Carson may be deduced from a comment in the *Times-Telephone* (July 31), noting that the architectural firm "has been in our city several weeks and drawn up several [plans]." Accompanying this statement was a list of some of the more modest homes going up. For a further confirmation one may have recourse to the *California Architect and Building News* (August 1884) in which the Newsoms listed some ten contracts in hand.

Carson selected another part of the site on which his current residence rested at Second and M Streets, occupying two city blocks and overlooking the Bay Mill which was providing the fortunes of the two partners. It was on the crest of a hill or knoll inclining upwards from the wharf and offering a sweeping view of the waterfront and littoral coast. It is said that he undertook the project at the particular time in 1884 partly to give employment to his mill hands during a slack period. At times Carson is reported to have had over 100 craftsmen, woodcarvers, and laborers on the job. A perusal of the local newspapers does disclose that at short intervals lumber companies were shutting down or laying off workers because of depressed prices or overproduction. Yet the same sources do record occasional shipments of lumber leaving for destinations elsewhere. In this connection it would seem inconsistent with the supposition of high rates of unemployment to accept the story often encountered that Carson brought in specialists from Europe. Rather the literature would suggest that the Scandinavians, Swiss, and Italians on the job were immigrants already settled in Humboldt County and engaged at their skilled trades, brought over by Carson to work in his mill. And many of the descendants of these craftsmen helped to develop the county's dairy farming industry.

Certainly, over the period of the construction of the Carson Mansion (1884-1885), many of the local citizens were not inhibited from building new homes and some quite expensive. Indeed, a *Weekly Humboldt Standard* supplement (May 2, 1885) presented a full page report street by street of the building boom since July 1884 although "many people complain of dull times." It reminded the community that "last fall the call for workmen was so great that the services of a carpenter could hardly be had for love or money." In its reference to Carson's residence the comment was that:

> "The style is Eastlake [;] it commands an excellent view of the surrounding country, will be thoroughly plumbed, in fact as nearly perfect, in every respect, as taste, skill, and money can make it, . . . [and] is said by some to resemble the Mark Hopkins residence in San Francisco [destroyed by the 1906 earthquake], with its cost estimated at not far from $50,000."

A similar sentiment is quoted in the *Weekly Humboldt Times-Tele-*

phone (January 31, 1885) from an article by a correspondent in the *San Francisco Chronicle* (January 18, 1885, p. 2, col. 5) to the effect that "another pioneer, William Carson, is building a residence which will cost over $20,000, and in style of architecture it strikingly resembles the San Francisco castle of Mrs. Mark Hopkins." A better idea of the cost may be gleaned from announcements in the *California Architect and Building News*. Under the heading of Building Intelligence, Miscellaneous, the issue of June 1884, p. 114 lists "a two-story and basement frame — day's labor — $25,000" and the issue of May 1885, p. 90 lists "additions — $50,000." What these figures mean as to such items as architects' fees, materials, landscaping, and any subcontractors is not clear but the total could well have run over $100,000.

Whether or not the community was fully aware of the cultural significance of the Carson project, commentaries are infrequent in the local newspapers and what there is reflected no penetrating architectural knowledge. On July 26, 1884 both the *Standard* and *Times-Telephone* made their initial observations. The former announced that "Carson's residence has been commenced [;] the location will make it a conspicuous landmark, and it will, in every particular, be one of the finest in Eureka." The latter announced that "the work of laying the foundation for Mr. Carson's new dwelling at the head of Second Street is fast approaching completion [;] it will be a large building and judging from the plans will be a handsome structure." It was not until the early fall of 1884 that the *Standard* made its next observations, noting on September 12 that "Carson's house will cost something over $80,000" and on October 6 that "the tower on Mr. Carson's new residence looms up from the lower end of Second Street [;] it will be the most elevated lookout in the city." The *Times-Telephone* had its say on November 11, noting that "the new residence of William Carson is assuming a handsome appearance [;] just now, the California Electric Company is at work running wires all through the building to be used for call bells, lighting gas, burglar alarms, etc. [;] when finished this will be the handsomest residence in the county and will be supplied with every modern convenience."

Nor did the further progress in construction draw any keener interpretations of the Carson residence. The *Times-Telephone* (December 17, 1884) noted humorously, perhaps referring to the devoutness of Carson, that "the arrow, the loftiest ornament... has been placed in position [;] it reaches a good ways in the direction of the good place, but if the earth turns round every 24 hours, its permanent indications are involved in some doubt." On January 24, 1885, the *Times-Telephone* reported its findings "as going to show the amount of labor yet to be performed... [and] it is asserted by those who know best that it will not be ready for occupation before July or August." Quite interesting was the jesting comment in the

Times-Telephone (May 1, 1885) for the inference that Carson was not a man to be trifled with. The passage was to the effect that "somebody without the fear of Mr. Carson, before his eyes, has dubbed the end of Second Street 'Knob Hill' [a reference to the exclusive residential district in San Francisco. Certainly], the elegant and elaborate mansion which is now being completed there makes the title a fitting one." On its part the *Standard* (July 20, 1885) observed that "a workman has arrived from San Francisco who will have charge of the construction of the main stairway of William Carson's fine residence [;] neither time nor money is being spared to make the edifice altogether complete."

The only instance of a conversation with Carson during the construction of the residence is passed on by the editor of the *Standard* (April 30, 1885). Carson described to him a piece of redwood timber that had been polished up at the cabinet makers' shop (along with an undertaking establishment) of Gemmill and Gibbard located "one block east of the Court House (about Second and K Streets)." It was treated with several coats of varnish, requiring only one more coat than mahogany to make it look equally beautiful. Though softer than mahogany, some parts of the redwood such as burls, crotches, and roots had a finer grain and "will be carefully worked up in the future instead of disposed as now." Carson added that he was considering the idea of fitting up the inside of some rooms in the new residence with it. If he did in fact carry out this thought, a strong likelihood could be those highly-polished redwood burls doing duty as pillars in the hallway of the second floor. That Carson was quite captivated by the possibilities may be deduced from an item in the *Times-Telephone* on August 20, 1886. Readers were urged to visit the office of Dolbeer and Carson where some of the "finest specimens of redwood knots ever in Eureka" were to be seen; [they] contain every variety of gnarl and when polished up by cabinet workmen are remarkably beautiful [;] many pieces of furniture are being made of these knots and the demand is increasing [;] they are not inferior in beauty to mahogany."

As a possible clue to the actual presence of the Carson family in their new home by the fall of 1885, there is the vague observation in the *Standard* (October 9, 1885) that "a good many hands are still employed on Mr. Carson's residence and the compliments that are passed on the elegance of the structure continue quite numerous." No less significant in fixing the chronology of the major completion of the Carson Mansion is an item in the *Times-Telephone* issue of November 4, 1885. The attention of the reader is called to an oil painting placed on exhibition in A. F. Weck's store window, a druggist and pharmacist who occupied premises at the corner of Third and F Streets in a building owned by Carson (destined to be replaced in 1891-1892 by a new structure housing the Ingomar Theatre). The artist was Roland Lee and the subject is "Dolbeer and Carson's mill from the waterfront, showing the vessels lying at the wharf loading, the mill and outbuildings, and the fine residence of William Carson in the background." It would indeed be gratifying if the thought expressed in the preface that this study might spur local inhabitants to share their past experiences were to come to fruition in the discovery of the canvas.

Perhaps the hesitation to devote greater space and publicity to the finale of the construction might have been out of deference to the current depression and the contrasts in poverty and wealth. Nor does there seem to have been any gala house-warming festivities by the Carson family itself, at least not reported for public consumption. At any rate, the account in Baird's data book report (1964) and repeated in a number of books that "the great house was begun in 1885 and completed in the early fall of 1886 . . . and occupied . . . in October 1886" would seem to be slightly off. The only references encountered in the *Times-Telephone* during 1886 refer to what may seem more like additional improvements. Specifically, the issue of August 15 records the arrival of a San Francisco man (C. B. Rutherford) "to superintend the commencement of the painting of William Carson's new house" and the issue of November 3 passes on the information that the "Gas Company recently extended its pipes to Carson's mills including Carson's residence."

In this connection, years later, perhaps in the 1960s, Andrew Genzoli, veteran reporter, raised an interesting point. It is contained in an undated and unidentified newspaper clipping in the *Fountain Papers* (vol. 28, p. 00221), but attributed to him in his column in the *Times* and worth repeating verbatim:

> While there are numerous photographs of the Carson Mansion since its completion, I have never seen a photograph of the home while it was under construction. Are photographs of this type in existence? Also in its life in the community? Like showing William Carson and his family being serenaded by the Eureka Cornet Band the day his lumber mill went on a ten-hour day.

A telephone call to Genzoli elicited the information that he had never received a single reply to his appeal.

Rather surprisingly it was the first issue of a short-lived newspaper, the *Humboldt Gazette* (April 25, 1887) which provided the most discerning appraisal in local circles. The article dealt with "Eureka's Progress" and stressed that for a population of 7,000 the figure of 257 buildings erected was an impressive accomplishment:

> Chief among the residences of the city lately completed is the elegant home of William Carson, Esq., and situated at the head of Second Street upon a broad plaza, it has a magnificent ocean view. It

will stand as a monument to a life of unexampled energy and honest integrity. Palatial in appearance, the interior is finished with rare and costly woods. It was built by day labor . . . and contractors estimate the value at not less than $75,000. It is prominent among the many magnificent suburban homes of California and few are its equal.

Landscaping

The landscaping of the grounds, for the residence was centered well back from the street, proved a matter of time. An excellent introduction into the subject may be found in Elinor Richey, *The Ultimate Victorians* (1970, pp. 20-27). As she would depict the Victorians in their homeland, they expended much thought and energy upon the task of an appropriate landscape. They liked to be ethically motivated and the cultivation of a garden taught the lessons of patience, endurance, and persistence. There would seem to have been three sanctioned garden arrangements. The Italian "formal" garden called for a geometric design of terraces and grass plots intersected with bordered walks and spaced with flowering urns, sculpture, and fountains. The English "natural" garden was a landscaped scheme which feigned an effect of natural growth with irregular settings of flowers, ferns, and shrubs in uneven clumps cut through by mossy paths. In its most extreme form of studied casualness the romanticism of wild and unfettered nature was sought, a garden all but concealed in a bosky dell of bushy thickets. The German "disciplined" garden was a landscape known as carpet bedding because the beds of plants and flowers were trimmed and ordered until they looked as smooth as a carpet. The beds were set amidst immaculate green lawns and given geometric shapes of circles, stars, triangles, and crescents, complete with contrasting colors and a ribbon border or narrow floral strip. All gardens afforded a wide choice of trysting retreats—latticed archways, weeping willows, rustic gazebos, vine-covered arbors.

In the case of the Carson Mansion, perhaps an acre of the two city blocks was landscaped. To begin with, a degree of privacy was achieved by an ornate wrought-iron fence which enclosed the grounds facing M Street and southward to Third Street. A recent acquisition to the photographic collection at the Humboldt State University Library (dated January 1902) discloses that a sidewalk constructed of wooden boards extended to the road along M Street. Also evident are the present-day two gates, a smaller one opening upon a concrete walk direct to the front porch and a wider one opening upon a paved driveway proceeding to the front porch along a curved path. But the picture of the home and grounds in Palmquist's collection of the photographs of A. W. Ericson, taken before 1890, suggests only one entrance into the grounds then and that a graveled walk circled around the house for access to the carriage house and stables. Furthermore, the lawn itself revealed grass growing wild and a rake resting upon a heap of collected leaves. However, a thickening of trees and bushes extending outward on the westerly edge of the residence does resemble the beginnings of what later became a miniature wooden area. More progress was made in 1902 as a photograph in the *Humboldt County Souvenir* (1902, p. 12 and 1904, 2nd ed., p. 15) discloses. The lawn is manageable and shrubs and bushes encircle the front and the south side where the other entrance into the house can be seen. Incidentally this photo shows two unidentified ladies on the front porch, conceivably Mrs. Carson and her daughter Carlotta (or a daughter-in-law).

The passage of years has witnessed, of course, the cultivation of a lovely landscape. Of the three sanctioned Victorian garden schemes, appearances would seem to lean towards an interpretation combining features of the English natural and the German disciplined gardens. The lawn in the front presents the illusion of a thick emerald velvet fabric. There is a large circular flower bed which seasonally may have azaleas, zinnias, marigolds, poppies, petunias, and violets. Skirting the base of the residence are rhododendron and camellia shrubs, lending further color in bloom to the picturesque home. The concrete walk to the porch is lined with manicured boxwoods and a yew tree stands guard at the foot of the steps. The miniature woods fronting towards the bay contains magnolias, palms, cypress, and pines. The miniature woods facing towards Third Street is deeper and possesses a more varied repertory of trees—Douglas firs, cherry, magnolias, palms, cypress, redwoods. In addition, one may encounter planted rows of annual and perennial flowers, hydrangea shrubs, and ferns. In the rear, to the back of the residence, still stands a woodshed of dimensions sufficiently ample to transform into a small apartment.

The Palmquist collection of A. W. Ericson's pictures show the outlines of a wooden fence farther back and the protrusion of what looks like a stable no longer in existence. Although not to be seen in most photographs, there is to the right of the woodshed the carriage house, now a garage for motor vehicles, with living quarters upstairs for an employee and his family. The previously-mentioned photograph of January 1902 fills in this gap, not only presenting the carriage house in full but also indicating that a small tower once adorned its roof. The large area to the rear of these structures now serves at the apparent pleasure of its owner as a parking lot. Yet another photographic acquisition at the Humboldt State University Library, chronicled as having been taken about the 1930s as an aerial shot, reveals that the owner of the lot used it to stockpile the products of his lumber mill. More recently the site has been acquired by the city and plans have been drawn up to develop this 2.3 acre parcel as a neighborhood of Victorian buildings containing offices, shops, and residences. The hope is to qualify for federal funds should an appropriate national measure be enacted.

Farther beyond the miniature woods facing towards Third Street is a fenced-in area which provided the Carson family with outdoor privacy. A tall growth of shrubbery—mainly ivy and holly—form an impenetrable shield against the curious walking along Third Street. Here the combination would appear to reflect a garden possessing features of both the English and the Italian approaches. There are a barbecue pit, a covered outdoor porch off the carriage house, and a trysting arbor fashioned of ivy. In the center there is a fountain area with an upright and weathered stone pedestal. Rose bushes line the wooden fence looking over the extensive parking lot. At intervals flower beds abound featuring marigolds, daisies, dahlias, petunias, and zinnias among many other species; the variety must be endless as the seasons come and go. Still another arrangement calls for a scattered orchard boasting here and there apple trees, crab apples, plums, and pears. For contrast there is heather, boxwood, privet, holly, and yew in varied sizes fashioning natural paths. Some accounts mention the reservation of an area as a vegetable patch. What sports were indulged in is a matter of conjecture. While the private garden did not possess a swimming pool during the span of the Carson generations, perhaps the horseshoe pits go back to their time. At any rate, little imagination is required to envisage the pleasantness of outdoor parties in fair weather.

Private gardens

Private gardens.

Pink Lady as seen from second floor balcony of Carson Mansion.

The Pink Lady by the light of the street lamp.

Close-up of Pink Lady "gingerbread."

CHAPTER FIVE

INGOMAR THEATRE: A MISSION

Carson Block

THE SECOND ACCULTURATION VENTURE of Carson was the construction of the Ingomar Theatre. But it must not be supposed that the realization of the project was a simple tale. The original purpose was to replace a two-story building which he had erected in 1872 at Third and F Streets to accommodate merchandise establishments and some professional offices. What he had in mind was a new structure providing expanded shopping space and many professional offices. More than this one would like to think that uppermost in his mind was a contribution to the improvement of the quality of life in Eureka. After all, the services necessary for material existence have some significance in nourishing human sensibilities and elevating the vision of a meaningful life. Eureka as the metropolis of Humboldt County merited the latest in modern building techniques and the opportunity seemed at hand to pioneer such a facility. Nor is the thesis far off that at the time the lumber business was suffering a depression and his mill hands could be kept employed to some extent. A perusal of the local newspapers for 1891-1892 would confirm the fact that the logging and milling industry was going through the throes of another slack period. The Carson Block could be a gesture of faith in the future of northern California.

Before proceeding with the story of the theater portion, the reader might find it interesting to know the overall facts about the Carson Block. The Newsoms were the architects as they had been for the Carson Mansion, a statement to be interpreted probably as Samuel and his sons. The estimated cost ranged between $100,000 and $115,000, plus an additional $30,000 for the completion of the interior of the theater. The year-end issue of the *Standard* (December 31, 1891) reviewed the state of construction and included a drawing of the facade on F Street. The straight and upright lines interspersed with arches at the lower level made a handsome front. The actual structure occupied 140 feet on Third Street and 110 feet on F Street. The building materials were redwood, brick, and tile. The ceiling timbers at the lower level were supported by wooded pillars, turned and ornamented, and finished in oil at Carson's mill. The walls were solid redwood six inches thick and as fireproof as brick. The outside finish at the lower level utilized pressed brick, tile facing, and large plate glass windows. The entrances to the stairways were fashioned with heavy arches of pressed brickwork. The spring of the arch in each case was made of tile and adorned with flower and vine designs. At each corner of the building there was a sort of round turret extending down from the edge of the sloping roof to the floor level of the second story, much like the oriel described in the Carson Mansion.

The two upper stories were reached by wide stairways finished in oak. Both the second and third floors had ample corridors, also finished in oak wainscoting, from which branched off smaller hallways containing the office entrances. There were fourteen offices on the second floor and thirteen on the third floor, some with bay windows. Eight offices on each upper floor were to have an additional backroom with storage space, closets, and amenities. In every office there would be a stationary washstand of the latest models with marble tops. Each office was to be fitted with radiators and have available both gas and electric lighting. The dental offices being prepared for contracted tenants had unusual new features, notably a drill to be powered by electricity instead of a pedal pump and new style wash basins fitted with nickel-plated pipes instead of plumbing connections covered with boards. The *Standard* concluded the review with the observation that when the building was finished it would be an imposing structure, "not only a matter of pride to its owner and to the county generally . . . [but also because] it is only the pioneer of a new architectural departure [in Eureka] . . . from the previous more transitory, gloomy, and fire-prone wooden structures."

The shops on the ground floor and the offices on the upper floors were ready for occupancy by July 1892. A. W. Randall Banking Company was located on the F Street side and gave its interior a luxurious touch with panels of burl and curly redwood. Equally impressive was the spacious store of Crocker Brothers, retailers of clothes and dry goods. Other tenants included Janssen and Company, dealers in fittings and furnishings, and a cigar and newsstand on Third Street leading to the offices on the upper floors. In its issue of October 27, 1892, the *Weekly Humboldt Times* noted that but few of the offices remained vacant. Somewhat humorously the editor referred to those on F Street as the Aesculapian Way with its tenanted disciples of the healing arts, those on the Third Street side as Blackstone Hall because of its legal inhabitants, and a suite isolated in the southeast corner of the building as "Mammon's Nook" for its occupant Charles Parsons (C. P.) Soule, cashier of the Bank of Eureka and later successor to William Carson as president. For a photograph of the Carson Block the reader is referred to the *Humboldt County Souvenir* (1904, 2nd ed., p. 147) and J. M. Eddy, *In the Redwood's Realm* (1893, p. 94).

A Playhouse Wanted

For the genesis of the theater portion of the Carson Block, one may well begin with the performance of a melodrama entitled *Octoroon* (or Life in Louisiana) in Russ Hall, a local "opera house," on the evening of Thursday, October 25, 1883. This play was written in 1859 by the well-known author and actor Dion Boucicault. It dealt with the explosive subject of slavery in the South. The plot revolved around the love between George Peyton, youthful heir to the plantation of his late uncle, and a supposed free mulatto girl by the name of Zoe (actually the illegitimate daughter of his uncle and raised as a white woman). In response to George's proposal of marriage, Zoe answered fearfully and woefully that the law in Louisiana forbade such an interracial union between a white man and a "tainted" Negress. What brought on a crisis was the proposed auction of the plantation to satisfy the claims of creditors, the consequence of the nefarious manipulations of a former overseer (McCloskey) who had his villainous heart set upon the possession of Zoe. As a means to thwart the prospective destitution of George Peyton, her lover, Zoe sought (but vainly) to bring about a marriage between him and a neighboring wealthy young white heiress. In the end, the timely receipt of a debt owed by an English firm kept the property in the Peyton family. In the meanwhile, a despondent Zoe, sold to the ex-overseer as a reclassified slave and shorn of any prospect of union with George Peyton, committed suicide by taking poison.

The reader is referred for a copy of the play to Arthur Hobson Quinn, ed., *Representative American Plays from 1767 to the Present* (New York: 1953, 7th ed.). Interestingly, when the play was produced on the London stage in the fall of 1861 a happier conclusion was provided allowing Zoe to escape her prospective enslavement and to marry George Peyton. The explanation would seem to have been that in England the sympathy of the upper class was with the South in the American Civil War and so the rationale of a better image for the Confederacy might be cultivated throughout the country if a less foreboding finale was provided. Whether the Eurekan audience had any deeper thoughts than that of mere entertainment can only be conjectured. Certainly, in 1883, the future of the newly-emancipated Negro population was very much in the public eye. And, apart from the moral and humanitarian principles involved for a society dedicated to egalitarianism, the concerned citizen might well draw the lesson that the dignity of free labor was a better foundation for a progressive nation.

The *Times-Telephone* followed closely the preparations of the Humboldt Dramatic Club. For the several weeks prior to the presentation of *Octoroon*, space was devoted to assure the community that the home talent would be equal to the challenging task. The issue of September 24 passed on the information from knowledgeable persons that the performance would surpass anything heretofore attempted. Stress was placed upon the fact that the leading roles were in the hands of especially capable individuals, notably Miss Lucy A. Huntington as Zoe and Louis T. Kinsey as McCloskey. At the time, in real life, the former pursued the career of a school teacher and the latter the post of county clerk. The issue of October 21 spelled out the scheduled details, the date to be Thursday, October 25, the price of general admission as fifty cents and reserved seats at seventy-five cents, and the ticket office located at the post office newsstand. The issue of October 25 contained the names of the full cast and with the thought of possibly recalling past kinsfolk for present-day descendants the rest of the actors and actresses are listed in alphabetical order: A. J. Bledsoe, Miss Carr, David Cutten, Charles Dauphiny, D. Foley, Theodore Fuller, Fred H. Gibson, George Gibson, Miss Clara Hall, F. Inman, J. E. Janssen, Harry Kelley, James B. Lent, H. A. Libbey, John Gallagher Murray. All were gifted, a perusal of local newspaper files disclosing their frequent participation in civic, church, and charitable programs as singers, readers, thespians, and elocutionists. And their occupations reflected all walks of life—public servants, school teachers, attorneys, merchants, insurance agents, music instructors, and housewives, to mention but a few.

The major review in the *Times-Telephone* was contained in the issue of October 27. The audience was estimated to be one of the largest ever gathered together in Eureka for such an affair. While the play "will always be a favorite with the theater-loving public," the crowd was really drawn "principally to greet the Humboldt Dramatic Club once more, that organization having won a place in the hearts of the people and established a reputation for producing works of merit in an artistic manner." Pleading restricted space, the critic wrote that the different roles were well sustained, "speaking naught in malice and bestowing praise where praise and credit is due." Even at that, an effort was made to single out individually the members of the cast and commend each for his or her interpretation of the parts assigned. But most pertinent for the heading of this section of the chapter was the last paragraph which should be read with the awareness of the physical shortcomings in staging a play in Eureka:

> "The stage in Russ Hall is rather small, and to produce such a piece in anything like a creditable manner without the necessary 'props,' scenes, etc., requires considerable ingenuity. The obstacles were [to be sure] all overcome.... [And one] hopes that the Club will soon make arrangements for other and several entertainments during the winter season, as their efforts uniformly give more and greater satisfaction than any of the traveling combinations that visit this section."

For the full illumination of the embarrassing incident that occurred during the performance one must read the post-mortem editorial in the *Times-Telephone* on November 1, 1883. Apparently the difficulty encountered with a cabin setting had been "laughable to all but those who had to deal with the exigencies of the play." Scenic effects had been nigh impossible on the small stage and "a really excellent performance was marred by the deficiencies of the space behind the footlights." This reference to the cabin setting had to do with the fifth act and at a moment of great solemnity. The specific lamentation of the editor related to "the ludicrous efforts of Dido [a Negress servant to the heroine Zoe] to enter her quarters and [unfortunately] to pull the cabin in after her [on the] mission to get her mistress some medicine which proved to be the suicidal poison."

The determination of the *Times-Telephone* to espouse the need for an adequate theater was made known as early as the issue of October 12, 1883. Presumably members of the *Octoroon* cast were already complaining during the period of rehearsals of the difficulties in staging the scenes. So, in the "local item" column, the following paragraph was inserted: "Who Will Build a New Opera House? Russ Hall is sufficient for ordinary performances, but the city is large enough to support a first-class theater building. A good investment for some enterprising capitalist." Moreover, as an editorial on November 1, 1883 saw it, the case should be considered in the context of the drama as a civilizing agent. The legitimate theater exercised "an elevating and ennobling influence and... elegant theatres are evidences of refinement and culture."

Most vigorous in persuasion at an intellectual level was a *Times-Telephone* editorial on November 18 and worthy of verbatim treatment:

> "One of the most forcible reasons which may be urged for the necessity of building a new and modern theatre in this city is the

influence of the stage—we mean the legitimate stage—upon the moral tone and intellectual character of the community. The complaint is often heard that the legitimate drama is rarely seen outside of the large cities. There are any number of traveling companies who furnish an evening's pleasant pastime, but who produce nothing of the character to point a moral or afford useful instruction. The cause of this state of things is apparent. The accommodations outside of the large cities are usually so poor that the best plays of the greatest authors cannot be produced with any satisfaction to the actors or their audiences.... Where such is the case the moral tone of the community is elevated and the acquisition of knowledge constantly promoted. The influence of the stage has been felt and recognized in all ages. There is reason to believe that at the time of the highest civilization of the Greeks—the most highly cultured of the ancient peoples—the stage had reached a greater degree of perfection than it has ever attained in modern times and that it was the most influential means of education known to the Athenians. True they had not then a Shakespeare, and there is still no better reason why the stage of the present day should rival the school or the pulpit in teaching lessons of morality and disseminating useful information. This can only be the case where the legitimate drama is produced, and the legitimate drama can only be produced in commodious and convenient theatres. If there were a first-class theatre in this city the splendid theatrical companies from Wallack's, the Union and Madison Square, and the renowned and talented impersonators of Shakespeare's characters who delight San Francisco audiences would extend their tours to this place. Their influence for good would soon be appreciated and recognized by all but the most straight-laced and dogmatic opposers of secular amusement...."

That the editor was not prepared to relinquish his objective may be deduced from his return to the subject a year later (November 15, 1884). If the popular idea in Europe was true to a certain extent that Americans overworked and cared little for recreation, it could equally be said that "hidden somewhere in the Yankee character is a love of fun and a genuine appreciation of humor, ascending in the ratio of culture to the highest development of dramatic taste." This trait had found "its first expression in rudely constructed, barn-like halls where strolling minstrels enliven the Winter evenings." The next advance revealed itself "in comfortable if not elegant concert halls," reaching through gradual steps "the beautiful and luxurious theatre." This "artistic and dramatic growth we have attempted to sketch has been witnessed in this city—all but the last and best stage." The lack of such a facility "keeps good companies away and deprives us of first-class dramatic entertainments."

Lest he be accused of dealing in vague generalities, the editor proceeded in the issue of November 1, 1883 (and repeated in the issue of November 15,

1884) to give some estimates and figures for anyone seeking a reasonably profitable investment. A theater with a seating capacity of about 1,500, a large and commodious stage, beautiful scenery, and furnished with all modern improvements could be erected for $25,000. In the way of revenue, the opportunities were numerous. The dress circle and orchestra seats in some theaters were in sectional rows and could be taken out and so transform the interior into a spacious and lovely ballroom for a rent of $25 per night. For a similar fee of $25 it could be let as a meeting hall. Five theatrical performances should net a sum of $125. In addition, the provision of two stores on the ground floor could be leased for $25 each and five offices on the upper floor at $5 each. On a monthly basis as thus calculated the returns amounted to $250 or enough to liquidate the investment in due time. And any receipts above such conservative estimates could pay for the services of a manager and assistants. In short, the benefactor would obtain a fair yield on his capital and "provide the city with a suitable theatre wherein home and foreign talent may in a fitting manner 'hold the mirror up to nature'."

For an explanation of how Carson came to incorporate a theater in his building plans, it must be stressed that Carson himself had become a devotee of the stage. The indulgence may have come from trips to the east but more likely from his frequent stays in San Francisco. Apparently in the loneliest of evenings spent between business conferences he found relaxation in attending plays. Presumably his acquaintance with *Ingomar the Barbarian* dated from these sojourns. As will be seen in the next chapter this play had become part of the repertory of most companies in New York and San Francisco as early as 1852 and was performed time and again. The fact that Carson was able to assimilate a level of culture unfamiliar to a frontier life would seem a commentary on the belief that environment alone determines the ability of human beings to absorb a sense of refinement. Without much of a formal education he surmounted the numbing circumstances inherent in logging and milling operations. The days spent in the forest were not entirely a peaceful reverie among bull whackers, swampers, choppers, and chain tenders toiling and sweating amidst dust-laden air at straining tasks and with stubborn animals. Nor could he have found the company of the mill hands any more uplifting amidst the tension of whirring machines and the shrieking sounds emitted in their operation. Yet Carson did not succumb to indulgence with his workers in their relaxations of drink and profanity in the neighboring saloons.

To what extent Carson encouraged and assisted the recruitment of theatrical troupes from San Francisco for Eurekan performances is uncertain. In any instance, the occasions must have been infrequent for a voyage of some 220 nautical miles each way in rough seas and troublesome sand bars was not an alluring attraction. Then, too, the available sites—Russ Hall, Baird's Opera House, Pratt's Opera House—left much to be desired in the way of seating capacity, stage facilities, and audience comfort. Local dramatic groups furnished most of the entertainment, mainly a modest menu of comedy, farce, minstrels, and melodrama. It must have been a momentous event in 1886 when these amateurs agreed to perform the taxing roles in the play, *Ingomar the Barbarian*. That the effort at serious drama loomed large in the minds of those responsible (and one may hazard the guess that Carson was in the forefront) might be suggested by a comment in the *Times-Telephone*. In its issue of October 24, 1886 the announcement drew the response that "it has been some time since the public were favored in this manner and we feel that *Ingomar* will receive a warm reception."

During the months of November and December 1886 the *Times-Telephone* offered a running commentary upon the preparations "going forward . . . for a delightful entertainment at Baird's Opera House on the appointed evening." Confidence was expressed in the ability of the *"dramatis personae"* to meet the challenge for "many of our leading amateurs are named in the cast of characters." On one occasion (November 14) the editor would intrigue his readers by quoting the final words: "Two souls with but a single thought, Two hearts that beat as one," an anticipation of the synopsis to be given in the chapter devoted to the play. The public was urged to patronize the affair for, apart from *Ingomar* being a meritorious dramatic presentation, the proceeds would go to charity. Nor did the fact that the original date of Thanksgiving evening had to be cancelled dampen its enthusiasm. The columns of the newspaper were made available to provide the cast with due notice of rehearsals and the public with directions on where to purchase tickets. In the issue of December 17, on which night the event would take place, the bait was dangled that "all desirous of seeing something unusually interesting will not fail to come out . . . when and where will be made known what Parthenia's mother said in regard to the tender passion." Reassurance too was given that the costumes had come (from San Francisco) on the *City of Chester* the previous day and "everything is now in readiness for tonight."

For the last few issues of the *Times-Telephone* prior to the performance an advertisement was run detailing the price of seats and the availability of tickets at J. E. Mathews' news agency and book store, located in the lower story of the Masonic building at the corner of Second and G Streets. Included in the instructions were the names of the cast and their respective roles. The director and leading man as Ingomar was Louis T. Kinsey, now cashier of both the bank and the savings institution headed by

William Carson. The leading feminine role as Parthenia was taken by Miss Lucy A. Huntington, now the proprietor of a private school located at the corner of Fifth and E Streets. Her particular forte was elocution. Photographs of these two thespians are to be found in the Theatre Arts Collection at Humboldt State University Library. With the thought again in mind that amongst posterity the new faces might evoke the nostalgia of ancestral kinsfolk, the rest of the participants are listed in alphabetical order: Miss L. Atkinson, B. Bergen, A. H. Chope, J. L. Crichton, C. Freese, W. Greggs, J. McCarthy, S. A. MacDonald, Miss W. McFarland, John Gallagher Murray, Louis Persons, Miss M. Rellinger, B. Skinner, Harry Taylor, W. W. Taylor, Miss Annie Zane.

As previously stated the performance took place the evening of Friday, December 17, 1886, at Baird's Opera House, as a benefit for charity, the tariff being fifty cents for general admission and seventy-five cents for reserved seats. It would not be surprising if the full details revealed that Carson was a patron defraying the expenses, notably the cost of costumes and perhaps some counsel as to the direction of the play. The review in the *Standard* (December 18) was laudatory, reporting "a large and intelligent audience" as very enthusiastic over the manner in which the "home talent" had managed the difficult roles. Even more fulsome was the *Times-Telephone* (December 19), characterizing the dramatic effort "as highly gratifying to the large and appreciative audience who witnessed it.... The parts were well committed, no one's memory seeming in the least at fault, and the interest increased during the progress of the play as the cordial and repeated applause fully testified." While the *Times-Telephone* was generous in distributing encomiums, "where all did well, it is invidious to particularize," it would also say that "the leading parts were taken in excellent manner." One must hope that some deeper import was drawn from the plot and that the frequency of the audience approval did not interrupt the continuity of the histrionic effort.

Indeed, some thirty-plus theatergoers (but not including Carson for whatever reason) signed a petition requesting a second engagement. This was provided on Tuesday evening, December 21, again attended by a large audience despite disagreeable weather conditions and described as equally well received in the *Times-Telephone*, December 23, 1886. A similar summary review is to be found in the weekly *Western Watchman*, a short-lived local newspaper. Its issue of December 25, 1886 made note of audience appreciation at the second performance "by frequent applauds." Certainly "each part was well supported throughout . . . and as a whole will long be remembered by those who were in attendance." An historian of local dramatic activities, Frank Bernard Bettendorf, asserts that "Mr. William Carson was in the audience [whether at one or both of the performances] and was quite impressed by the work of the amateurs and was interested in the theme of the play itself as a civilizing influence." While he cites no specific sources, perhaps the answer might be provided in a senior seminar paper written at Humboldt State University by Lenny Escarda entitled, *The Ingomar Theatre* (1959). The paper refers to a tape recording by Mrs. Stanley Roscoe, an esteemed local historian, as the source for the story. A telephone conversation with this knowledgeable lady elicited the information that her source in turn was Mrs. Annie Zane Murray, school teacher and later the wife of a superior court judge (George D. Murray). She had a minor role among the Greek citizenry who had their fleeting moments of glory on the stage those two nights and was present when Carson sought out the cast and told them how delighted he had been with their performance and that it surely "deserved a theatre." Mrs. Annie Zane Murray is to remembered also, according to obituaries in June 1960, as the first president of the Humboldt County Historical Society.

Neither the impressive financial accountancy of two editorials nor the memory of the cultural experience with the *Ingomar* performances in 1886 faded completely from the thoughts of local citizens. When it first became known in the spring of 1891 that Carson contemplated the construction of a modern business and office building, he was urged to include a theater in his plans. The *Standard* (May 5, 1891) made a special plea:

> "Wanted—An Opera House. It is frequently remarked that it is to be regretted that a city like Eureka has no respectable Opera House. This fact is emphasized now while we have a first-class troupe in the city [Gage and Keene Company with a repertory including *Pygmalion and Galatea* and *Damon and Pythias*]. It is rumored that the new block to be erected on the corner of Third and F Streets will contain a first-class opera house capable of seating 1,400 people. Whether there is a good foundation for the rumor we do not know; but Mr. Carson will earn the gratitude of the people and add a much needed improvement to the city, if the rumor proves true."

Carson resolved to accept the challenge, spurred by his own interest in the theater and by a desire to show his confidence in Eureka's economy which was sagging at the time. The *Weekly Humboldt Times* (June 25, 1891), furnished with the preliminary plans, announced the decision in glowing words:

> "The building will be seventy feet in height, covering three stories with the lower floor given over to business stores and some offices on the second [and third] floor. The theatre is to occupy the entire eastern half of the building for the full height of the two [upper] stories. The roof over the theatre will be considerably higher than that of the other portions of the building and will be trussed and arched giving a high ceiling.

The auditorium will contain a balcony, dress circle, and parquette [orchestra circle], the floor being terraced as in all San Francisco theatres and will seat 1,400 people. Surrounding the theatre on two sides, corresponding with F and G Streets, will be a wide corridor into which will open the entrances, one, the main entrance from F Street and the other from Third Street between the two stores on that street. The box office will be located at the foot of the stairs at the F Street entrance. Owing to the manner of the arrangement of the interior of the theatre, it can be used for no other than theatrical purposes and accordingly will be furnished and fitted in the most approved style and provided with everything necessary to make it a first-class theatre in every particular...."

Construction

The sources for the theater portion are the *Standard* (December 12, 1892) and the *Times* (December 23, 1892). Their commentaries reflect a community engrossed in the project as if it were a civic enterprise. By the summer of 1892 the deep stage, huge balcony, green ceiling, and blue walls were taking shape in a way that indicated "nothing will be left undone to make this handsome Thespian temple as complete as possible." Decorators were brought in from San Francisco and it was heart-warming to hear such craftsmen who had done work in many other California theaters vouchsafe that "no theatre on the coast will be more handsomely finished than this." The facades of the gallery, boxes, and proscenium arch were to be covered with plaster casts made on the spot and the molds then broken. The sketches showed plans for intricate flower and vine designs with masked faces peeping out at intervals. Numerous openings were to be seen for the insertion of incandescent bulbs. In time the scenery equipment arrived from Chicago and along with it came the specialists to put everything in permanent place. And over the center of the proscenium arch a tablet was being prepared bearing the words: "Ingomar Theatre, Erected MDCCCXCII," one more testimony to Carson's admiration for the qualities of a play to be discussed in the next chapter. An ebullient editor was prompted to exult that the "Opera House will be one of the finest country theatres in the nation."

Not until December 1892 was the Ingomar Theatre prepared to schedule its first performance. The seats were truly regal in brocaded coverings and cost $25 each. Although a capacity of 1,400 had been rumored (and wanted), there were 837 fixed seats and improvisations could run the count to over 1,000. The main entrance was on F Street, embellished with several arches. Halfway up the broad stairway was the box office. At the head of the stairway were the double doors leading to the auditorium. Between the flights of stairs a cloakroom was available. A spacious hallway ran around the two sides of the auditorium. Inside, a short flight of steps at each end led to the foyer. The foyer itself was cut off from the main floor by a paneled partition of elaborate woodwork pierced for entry with arched and carved openings and fitted out with electric-blue plush draperies. The foyer possessed three elegant chandeliers with bracketed side lights to give the intimate room an almost daylight effect. The floor was carpeted with a moquet of soft wood-brown tone in perfect harmony with the surroundings. This carpeting was continued in the passageways. Lounges and chairs in leather upholstery were generously distributed about the foyer for the early arrivals.

The main floor of the auditorium was divided into two sections, the separation marked by a brass railing. The dress circle covered the rear portion while the orchestra extended forward to still another brass railing which established the orchestra pit. The rows of chairs were set in semicircles and rose in an incline sufficient to allow every one to command an unobstructed view of the stage. The aisles were neatly carpeted in the same soft wood-brown tones as in the foyer. The rows of seats were set apart so that an individual had ample room to reach his seat. Passage to the gallery and the enclosed boxes was up another flight of stairs available at both ends of the foyer. The same care was taken to assure the comfort of those in the gallery (balcony). Every seat was claimed to have a clear view of the stage and every musical note from the orchestra and every spoken word from the stage was to be plainly audible. The dome of the ceiling was high enough to obviate any sensation of the gallery being hemmed in or to suggest any sense of squalidness. The ventilation was so well managed that the air circulated "as sweet and pure in the gallery as downstairs."

The *Times* (December 23, 1892) carried proudly on the front page the account of what its reporter sensed personally the opening night upon stepping through an archway onto the main floor. In addition, the issue included sketches of the Carson Block and the interior looking out from the stage towards the gallery and vice versa:

> "One enters into the full blaze and glory of the Ingomar Theatre—a glory that is all its own and much easier to see and to enjoy than to describe. The eye finds so much that is attractive and alluring that it wanders from point to point, not knowing where to begin its work of critical inspection. The color tone of the decorations (cream and gold) is perfect—the fact is mentally jotted down, so is the light, so are the designs on the ceiling and wall . . . and balcony facing; so are the brass railings about the proscenium boxes and the orchestra, and stage; so are the comfortable seatings; so in fact is everything, and finally the eye rests a moment on the handsome drop curtain, which is

a Roman scene with the Tiber flowing peacefully across the middle distance, and a broad roadway in the foreground. On either side are the rich folds of a great curtain looped back to show the pretty picture. Then the eye goes back again to wall and ceiling, hoping to become familiar with the details of the beautiful work. . . .

 Mr. Carson is to be congratulated on having produced a perfect theatre. . . ."

On each side of the stage were the boxes, ten in number, distributed in clusters of five—four open boxes elevated above the level of the main floor plus an enclosed box at an upper level. Each of the open boxes was arranged to seat four persons and each enclosed box had accommodations for eight persons. The edges of the boxes were fitted with fabric and ornamented with finely-hammered brass railings. The interiors were commodious and well furnished, the seats being of burnished brass with plush upholstery. Smaller arches, extending well out over the auditorium, formed with their decorative and rich drapings the passageways to the boxes.

The designs for ornamentation were in foliage, fruits, and flowers. The proscenium arch sported floriate designs, the tinting and gilding being exquisitely delicate. On the arched front of each enclosed box there was a large entablature bearing a lion's head surrounded by foliage. The front of the gallery was profusely decorated in fruit and leaf patterns and the grotesque masks peeping out at intervals were remindful of medieval gargoyles. The walls boasted similar decorations of gilded and tinted foliage and the bracket chandeliers along the sides were marvels of beauty in brass and crystal. The ventilator in the ceiling was covered by a centerpiece over eight feet in diameter from which hung suspended a brilliantly-lighted chandelier. Throughout the interior the illuminating effect was to diffuse a circle of soft radiance. If the theater has been described as classical in its architectural style, one could discern also a touch of the rococo.

The stage was good-sized as comparisons went in those days, some 30 by 35 feet and without pitch. The incandescent bulbs were sunk below the stage level and consisted of red, white, and blue lights, each color being on a separate circuit. The border lights carried the same three colors, each with its own circuit. There were two flashlights, so arranged as to be available at any spot on the stage. A handsome brass railing marked the point inside which the curtain rested when unfurled. Much pride was manifested in this drop curtain which lifted bodily without rolling, a magnificent work of art not excelled anywhere on the coast. Side arches next to the lower level open boxes gave access to rounded stands, one at each end of the main arch, from which encored members of the cast could bow their thanks when "called before the curtain." In the *Dolbeer-Carson Business Papers* (volume 2, p. 101), there is recorded for December 1892 the purchase of "one square grand Knabe piano with stool and cover for the Ingomar Theatre, $575.00."

Behind the footlights the details were no less complete. All the lights were managed from a switchboard located on the left side directly over the dynamo in the basement. Here too were the speaking tubes leading to the basement, orchestra pit, and the stage. Above the stage was an immense "vault" into which the scenery was lifted. Every scene, wing, and fly showed the forethought of skilful workmen brought in from Chicago to make the permanent arrangements. On the right side there was a flat where all the ropes and pulleys were managed while on the left side was a corresponding flat to be used for scenery painting. The stage was furnished with the latest type of traps.

The dressing rooms were at the level of the main floor and reached by easy steps from the stage. Those for the ladies were to the right and provided with every convenience for comfort. To the left and beneath the stage level were the quarters for the gentlemen—a general dressing room and four smaller ones, equally complete in details and accessibility. The space beneath the stage proper was allocated to the usages of the carpenter and the property man. The three traps were worked from this subterranean area. Here also the members of the orchestra gathered at intermission. This region was reached by a stairway from the so-called Opera Alley at the back of the building.

Every precaution was taken against fire. Automatic hose reels were posted about the theater, the hose and pipe always coupled for readiness at an instant's notice. Everything back of the footlights was treated with an asbestos fire-proofing material. The doors swung outward so that no jam could occur in the case of panic. The structure was particularly safe against fire because the redwoods were not, of course, a combustible wood. There were four exits, one at the main entrance, another at the angle of the hallway, and the other two off from the stage at opposite ends. In addition, there was still another exit from the dressing rooms to Opera Alley which served equally as an entrance for the performers. For photographs of the interior of the Ingomar Theatre see the *Humboldt County Souvenir* (1904, 2nd ed., p. 147) and the Theatre Arts Collection in the Humboldt State University Library.

That the popularity of the playhouse was instantaneous might be inferred from a cabinet photograph. It was distributed with the compliments of the Wunderlich Brothers, photographers, just as free calendars are now offered to customers of business firms. This particular one contained five insets, the two brothers, the Carson Block exterior, the stage and the curtain drapes, a view of the main floor and balcony from the stage, and a view of the lower boxes and the upper loge on the right side from the

Carson Block.

Ingomar Theatre.

Ingomar Theatre from stage.

Ingomar Theatre.

Close-up of enclosed box at upper level.

Ingomar Theatre lower (open) boxes.

vantage point of the audience. This cabinet photograph is in the Steenfott folder in the special collections room of the Humboldt State University Library.

Opening Presentation

For the opening presentation of the Ingomar Theatre a professional company was sought to perform *Ingomar*. Negotiations were undertaken to have the L. R. Stockwell Company do the play with Eleanor Barry in the main female role. But the impresario in San Francisco was unable to assemble a cast for the trip to Eureka. Instead a local dramatic society in rehearsal for a play scheduled the next spring entitled *The Golden Giant*, centered in an Idaho mining camp, was substituted. Both Carson and the manager of the theater, Willard Wells (Wells and Son's Drug Store located at Second and F Streets) were loathe to leave the theater closed during the Christmas holidays. The *Standard* (December 12 and 17, 1892) expressed confidence that the new crop of amateur thespians under the direction of Louis T. Kinsey would perform in first-class fashion and with appropriate costumes. The editor averred that "it is an event in the history of Eureka and marks a new era of progress and civilization for this city and county."

The momentous event took place on the evening of December 22, 1892. The house was reported as full when the orchestra played the "Siege of Paris" and the audience responded with loud applause. Apparently from modesty and shyness William Carson remained in the foyer (or perhaps a suite of offices which he retained for himself in the Carson Block) until the conclusion of the dedicatory speech "and the danger of personal allusion was passed." Nevertheless, upon entering his box, the ovation which he received was ample proof that Eureka appreciated his contribution. Previously the speaker's reference to him as a benefactor in providing this beautiful "Temple of the Muses" had prompted a veritable outburst of cheers.

The dedicatory speaker was Alonzo Judson Monroe (a tenant in the Carson Block) whose legal practice included terms as district attorney of Humboldt County and city attorney of Eureka. His oratorical ability was availed of often by the community on civic occasions. He was also a participating thespian in his own right. His speech, lengthy as it is, and not dissimilar in substance to the editorial in the *Times-Telephone* (November 18, 1883), merits verbatim treatment for its confirmation of the civilizing theme as being uppermost in the mind of William Carson (*Times*, December 23, 1892):

"It is with mingled feelings of gratification and pride that we tonight dedicate this beautiful house to the purpose for which it was built. Eureka can now boast of one of the finest theatres in the state. We are gratified that we at last have an opera house, and we feel a pardonable pride in one so beautiful, so elegant and so complete. Our pleasure is highlighted by the thought that as this theatre was built for public use it is ours; that we can speak of it . . . as our 'New Opera House.' We rejoice that we can refer to it as a proof of our development and progress as a city. It is apparent when we consider that the building of this theatre is not a mere business proposition. It is a contribution from a public-spirited citizen to his fellow citizens and to the city's growth; a munificent gift for which all are sincerely grateful to one of our big-hearted, leading men—William Carson.

This dedication marks an auspicious time in our history. The spirit of progress is abroad. Eureka is putting on the garb of a modern city. The obstructions to our bar [the entry to the harbor] are being removed and we look forward with confidence for improved facilities of travel to the metropolis of the state. And now, we can be reasonably assured that leading actors and companies that visit our coast will not continue to pass us by.

Ingomar Theatre is the name given by Mr. Carson, and it is most appropriately bestowed. You remember that Ingomar is represented as a barbarian, who was ennobled by the refining power of woman and elevated by the influence of civilization. This theatre stands on the western verge of the Union. It is erected at a point where barbarianism made its last stand against the westward march of civilization and empire [regrettably a typical view then of the dilemma of the American Indian]; and erected by a pioneer who bore the burdens and toils of early days [William Carson]. In the light of the past and the circumstances attending this dedication, which marks an advance of this city along the lines of progress and culture, it will be admitted that the word 'Ingomar' has been happily applied.

The parts in the play to be acted to-night are taken by the members of the Comrades Amateur Dramatic Company of this city. It was intended that one of the best companies of the day should open the theatre by the rendition of 'Ingomar', but as a company could not be obtained at this time, the Comrades Company were invited to open the house, and they accepted the invitation. The company were rehearsing the play you are to see to-night, intending to present it in the spring, after the theatre had been formally opened. Had the company known that they should open this theatre, a different and special play would have been selected, and much more preparation made than has been possible in the short time since the invitation was received. The Comrades is an amateur company organized not for profit, but for social pleasure and culture on literary and dramatic lines. While all regret that stars are not to shine here on the opening night, it is not inappropriate that this theatre, built by one of our own citizens, should be dedicated by our own people. The Comrades ask your indulgence for all defects, remembering that they are not professionals, and that you will graciously pass their imperfections by.

[Turning to the broader subject of the theater in the spectrum of civilization, Monroe continued thus.] The theatre has existed in some form in all ages, and among all the tribes and races of men. It is a necessity in our day as a means of occasional recreation and relaxation to those who endure the strains of modern society. It displaces other forms of amusement less entitled to popular support.

The theatre counteracts the tendency of the age toward the practical and towards a surrender of the ideal; a tendency most noticeable in new communities engrossed in developing natural resources like the one in which we live. The aspiration and struggle for the ideal is the principle of everything high and worthy in human life. The true function of the theatre is while it entertains, to minister, amid the sordid realities of human life, to that love of beauty and goodness which dwells in all human hearts; to keep alive and aglow that love of the ideal which is a necessary attribute of lofty character.

The stage has called into existence the greatest and noblest literature produced by human mind. It has exerted a powerful influence in the refinement of public taste and manners. The theatre more than all other causes preserves the purity and elegance of the language.

The greatest attraction of the theatre is in its exhibitions of the emotions and passions of the human heart. Man has forever stood on the shore of being unable to fathom the mystery of the soul. On the very threshold of his enquiries he is baffled and thrown back upon himself. This is beautifully illustrated from the tragedy of Ion [who in Greek mythology], asked by Clementhe, 'Shall we meet again?', replies:

'I have asked that dreadful question of the hills
That look eternal; of the flowing streams
That lucid flow forever; of the stars
Amid whose fields of azure my raised spirit
Hath trod in glory; all were dumb; but now,
While I thus gaze upon thy living face,
I feel the love that kindles through its beauty,
Can never wholly perish; we shall meet
Again Clementhe.'

The great telescopes have carried men's vision far into the outlying regions of infinite space. The microscope has revealed to him the myriad of life of a world invisible to the unaided eye. He has discovered the forces that move the heavenly bodies and keep them forever in their appointed paths. With electric fire he flashes messages beneath oceans to distant continents and sends his spoken words on wings of flame to listening ears. In nearly every department of human enquiry his 'exploring mind has brought bright gems from the caves of knowledge.' The mystery of the soul, more than all else, he cannot search out or understand. And yet this is the most interesting and absorbing field of his enquiry and thought. We are irresistibly attracted by the workings of the soul, as shown in man's struggles, his hopes and aspirations; his triumphs, his disappointments and defeats; his joys and his felicity; his sins, his remorse, his agony and his despair. These subjects, so profoundly interesting, give the theatre a permanent hold on the popular mind. The stage presents them in a realistic form, thus entertaining, instructing, and enforcing the lessons of wisdom and truth.

Its patrons make the theatre what it is. They are responsible if it fails to exert a refining and elevating influence. Let us remember our responsibility and patronize only such productions as are worthy of our support. In that way we will surely show our appreciation and respect for the generous citizen, who has built for us 'Ingomar Theatre.'"

Not too much in the way of a spirited review of *The Golden Giant* is to be found in the local newspapers. Still again for the enlightenment of posterity who may be able to identify among the new crop in the cast past kinsfolk the roster is as follows: "Jack Thurston, Lawrence F. Puter, Otto C. Gregor, A. J. Monroe, Mr. Hall, H. S. Richardson, Little Lulu Richardson, Miss Rhoda Chase, Miss Clara Hanna, Mrs. (Henry) Way, Mrs. R. Young." Besides commending "the performance of the amateurs," the *Times* (December 23, 1892) offered a very condensed synopsis of the play:

"It is one of the strongest of modern dramas, and calls for a very wide range of histrionic ability. The plot is based upon incidents of mining camp life, and while the play deals largely with that phase of life, it also furnishes a glimpse of upper-tendom as seen in New York."

Besides commending "all characters for their acting and speaking," the *Standard* (December 23, 1892) offered also a synopsis although more fully developed as follows:

"the curtain rises on a mining scene in Idaho. In the distance are snow-capped mountains and in the foreground a canyon where lay the Golden Giant mine. A stage accident occurs near the camp. The Golden Giant, who takes his nickname from the mine which he owns, is introduced to the audience with the heroine in his arms, having rescued her from the river where she was thrown. She is the wife of a partner in the mine who is supposed to be dead. Golden Giant steps in to protect her from the heavy villain who is trying to get possession of her interest in the mine. After seven years in the madhouse her husband is released and seeks revenge on Golden Giant but is killed by the heavy villain. The Golden Giant marries the heroine but is poisoned by the heavy villain against his wife and goes in exile to Europe for several years. Upon his return the heavy villain seeks to kill him but a gambler who is courting Golden Giant's sister despite her brother's disapproval of him intervenes to slay the heavy villain. In his dying moments the latter confesses the falsity of his evil gossip against the wife of Golden Giant. The finale finds Golden Giant and his wife reconciled and his sister married to the gambler [hopefully reformed]."

In short, the Eurekan audience was left to discover for itself what morality, lesson, or homily could be extracted from the melodrama.

Somewhat confused by these local synopses of the play, I sought further information from the curator of the Harvard Theatre Collection housed at the Harvard College Library. While the reply expressed regret at the inability to locate a copy of the play itself, several reviews were enclosed of early performances—Boston *Courier* (December 11, 1887), Providence *Bulletin* (October 9, 1888), Philadephia *Item* (December 23, 1888). A second source of inquiry was the Serra Regional Library System whose reply was no more comforting. Neither did it find a copy and did not think it was ever formally published. But it also submitted a review of a performance at the Fifth Avenue Theatre in New York City by the *New York Times* (April 12, 1887, p. 5, col. 1). Possibly the failure to turn up a copy may be owing to the lack of a copyright law (until 1892), prompting playwrights to withhold publication because of the widespread practice of piracy.

Comparisons between these early presentations and that in Eureka in 1892 would indicate that over the several years alterations were constantly being introduced. If the summaries in the Eureka newspapers are accurate, the most notable difference would seem to do with the first husband of the heroine—a partner of the Golden Giant in the Idaho mine of the same name. The earlier formats have the villain producing a twin brother of the first husband as the genuine article come to life and so deprive the Golden Giant as the second husband of his wife. Again, the earlier formats identify the scene in which the Golden Giant rescues the heroine at the outset of the play as the upsetting of the stagecoach as it crosses over a bridge, causing the heroine to fall into the stream. The fact emerges that the heroine was fleeing from her east coast abode where the villain had been pressing her to sign over interest in the mine in her capacity as the widow of her deceased first husband. Still again, the earlier formats describe the particular scandal which the villain related to the Golden Giant (sufficiently shocking to send the disillusioned bridegroom off to Europe) as his own "sort of guiltless but compromising elopement with the partner's wife [the heroine]" in the bygone past. As for the so-called confession of the dying villain that his story was false, the earlier formats have the henchman of the villain, in a state of inebriation, divulging the evil machinations of his master.

Incidentally, while the United States copyright office lists the five-act dramatic composition (April 19, 1884, No. 8244) in the names of Clay

Greene and McKee Rankin, the east coast reviews identify the former as the author and the latter's wife as the leading actress. She takes the secondary role of the Golden Giant's sister (virtuous but lacking in the adventitious graces of manners and refinement) rather than that of the heroine. What comes forth in these earlier formats is simply a western drama representative of the rough-and-tumble characters typical in the mining camps of the Bret Harte genre. Incidentally Bret Harte himself lived for a time in Arcata where he was known as Frank Harte and taught school. At best the search for a moral lesson could be reduced to the *cliché* that "good guys win out in the end" and "villains meet their just fate."

CHAPTER SIX

INGOMAR THE BARBARIAN: A CATALYST

Introduction

THE TIME HAS COME to deal with the contents of the play which had spurred Carson to envisage a modern theater as a civilizing influence in Humboldt County. The author was Friedrich Halm, the pen name of Baron von Münch-Bellinghausen (whose father had served as a councillor of state in the reign of Emperor Francis II of Austria). It was written in 1842 and bore the title of *Der Sohn der Wildniss*. While there is an earlier translation in English by Charles Anthon, a New Yorker, in 1848, called *The Son of the Wilderness*, the best known version adapted for the stage was by Maria Lovell, a London writer. Her selection of *Ingomar the Barbarian* as the title may well have been motivated by its "catchiness." *The William Warren Edition of Standard Plays*, published by the Walter H. Baker Company, Boston, 1896, has an especially informative introduction about the early productions and performers. Indeed, the edition was made from the prompt-book of Julia Marlowe (Taber). It is interesting to know that for some seasons she played the piece in four instead of five acts, omitting act four which is a duet between the hero and the heroine. The costumes worn by members of the cast are described in detail, probably as a guide for new productions. More than this, the edition spells out at the appropriate moments during the play the lighting effects to be used, the trumpet calls, the noises and the cries to be made, and the occasions for music, besides the usual directions for entrances, exits, and curtain shifts.

The initial presentation took place in London during June 1851 at the

Drury Theatre. James Anderson was not only manager but leading man and Miss Vandenhoff filled the role of leading woman. Shortly afterwards, on December 1, 1851, the play was produced at the Broadway Theatre in New York, starring Fred B. Conway and Mme. Ponisi. The play also opened on the same evening at the Bowery, starring Edward Eddy and Mrs. Edward Parker (née Amelia Sylvia). It ran for two weeks at each house, the comment on the Bowery presentation with a less well-known cast being "its pseudo-classicism perhaps did not please Shirtsleeves in the pit or peanuts in the gallery." Thereafter the play was given frequently and in other cities along the eastern seaboard. An examination of the annals of the New York stage discloses that rarely a year passed without its revival and more often there were two or three productions in the same year. The total for the New York stage from 1851 to 1901 must have come close to three score productions and on some occasions for extended engagements. The most fruitful books in the bibliography are those by Brown, *A History of the New York Stage* (1903); Ireland, *Records of the New York Stage from 1750 to 1860* (1866); and Odell, *Annals of the New York Stage* (1949).

The list of actors and actresses who took the leading roles as Ingomar and Parthenia reflected its popularity in the second half of the nineteenth century. On November 2, 1852, at the Broadway Theatre, the featured performers were Julia Dean and Fred B. Conway and they repeated their respective roles subsequently with other partners for the next two decades. The appearance of Tomasso Salvini, noted Italian actor, on September 22, 1873, was accompanied with the observation that "his superb physique was specially suited," a model of true realism for the enactment of Ingomar. Mary Anderson commenced her professional career as Parthenia in November 1877 and did it again in November 1878 at the Fifth Avenue Theatre. She was particularly commended for her classic beauty and exquisite profile, marking her out as most closely associated with the virginal purity of the Grecian maiden. Indeed, she chose the play for her debut in London on September 1, 1883 at the Lyceum Theatre. Julia Marlowe likewise began her professional career in the role of Parthenia in the autumn of 1887 at New London, Connecticut, and an engagement followed on October 20, 1887 at the Bijou Theatre. Among other well-known theatrical figures who found the play challenging were Harry A. Perry, John Edward McCullough, Eben Plympton, and Robert Downing as Ingomar and Anna Cora Mowatt, Mary Provost, Minna K. Gale, and Jean Davenport as Parthenia.

The annals of the San Francisco stage were no less impressive for the frequent presentations of *Ingomar*. The best books on the list in the bibliography are Gaer, *The Theatre of the Gold Rush Decade in San Francisco* (1935); Gagey, *The San Francisco Stage* (1950); and McMinn, *The Theater of the Golden Era in California* (1941). One can envisage Carson on business trips to the Golden City looking forward to attendance at his "favorite stage play." Certainly the advent of leading thespians from the east on the Pacific coast must have stirred considerable excitement among devotees of the stage. The earliest engagement would seem to have been in the spring of 1852, the cast headlined by Mrs. James Stark (née Sarah Kirby). A charity performance was included, at which Mrs. Stark was presented with a "rich cluster of diamonds set in a ring, and a massive gold bracelet." In the spring of 1855 Jean Davenport offered her interpretation of Parthenia. In 1856 Julia Dean and Mary Provost were rivals in parallel productions. Mary Anderson and John Edward McCullough were coupled as appearing "in early days at the Old California Theatre [perhaps in 1876]." Tomasso Salvini included the play in his repertory on a visit to San Francisco in February 1886. Julia Marlowe scheduled a tour to San Francisco in 1892 and performed the role of Parthenia. A veteran in terms of appearances on the California stage was Nance O'Neill, still being billed as the female lead as late as the winter of 1898-1899.

Synopsis

Turning to the play itself, the scene is set in Gaul a century after the founding of Massilia (Marseilles) by Phoenician traders. By the time the action takes place it has become a Greek colony pursuing a pastoral and tilling economy. It is governed by a leader called the Timarch. The immediate crisis relates to the family of a poor armorer by the name of Myron. His shrewish wife Actea is eager to have their lovely daughter Parthenia ease the rigors of their declining years by marrying the widower Polydor, a greedy and grasping merchant. Despite her mother's pleas, Parthenia spurns Polydor on the ground that she does not love him. Her reply to him leaves little doubt as to her hostile feelings:

> "An answer thou shalt have, and mark it well. Procure your children, sir, a schoolmaster, at any price, and whence you please! A slave to guard your house, attend to bolts and bars. Shouldst thou fall sick, there at the corner yonder, Go, bid the huckster sell thee wholesome herbs; Mix for thyself thy medicine and drink. But know for me there grows no bitter herb on earth than sight of thee, thou poor, heartless miser."

To make matters worse, the poor armorer is taken prisoner by a band of the Alemanni, a nomadic German tribe, and reduced to the status of a slave. The Timarch refuses to go to his rescue, asserting that his responsibility is only to defend citizens within the walls of the city. No less discouraging is the refusal of neighbors to pay the ransom for his release. In desperation

Parthenia determines to offer herself to the Alemanni in redemption for the freedom of her father.

The second act opens with Parthenia brought before Ingomar, young chieftain of the Alemanni band. She pleads for the return of her father, pledging that she would "do more work than twenty pining slaves." She could spin and weave, prepare meals, sing sweet songs, and tell brave tales. Ingomar agrees that it would be a good exchange and sets the old man free.

However, Parthenia quickly lets Ingomar know that she does not regard herself as a slave but rather as a hostage. Furthermore, in performing chores she assumes the role of a frank exponent of Greek ways. She prepares garlands of field flowers, noting that the sight gladdens the eye and the scent refreshes the body. She derides the German practice of bargaining for brides in the coinage of cattle. Her songs are designed to awaken the sense of beauty. A bewildered Ingomar has no answer for a situation seemingly unmanly. Indeed, before long, Ingomar gathers the flowers and assists in the domestic duties. Subtly but surely the darts of Cupid are piercing the crust of barbaric masculinity.

The third act finds the band of Alemanni restless and surly over the new state of affairs. Daily they press upon Ingomar the urgency to break camp and to move on against the troublesome Allobrogi tribe. They blame the Greek girl for their leader's dalliance and plot to sell her as a slave to a trading vessel from Carthage. Ingomar wrestles with his conscience, belaboring himself for succumbing to the wiles of a woman. He pleads with Parthenia to be his companion in arms against the Allobrogi. She upbraids him for seeking to resume the life of a "rude forest's outlaw son, a savage, a barbarian desolator of the fair land—a cattle stealer." But when the Alemanni band endeavors to carry out their scheme to sell her into slavery Ingomar intervenes. As a settlement he surrenders his fifth part of the spoils from future raids in return for her freedom. As a final gesture Ingomar insists upon acting as guide and protector for her journey back to Massilia.

The fourth act projects Parthenia and Ingomar plodding their way onwards through the forest. She is overjoyed at the prospect of the sight of her homeland and sings the praises of Greek life. He challenges the vaunted superiority of yonder city "with polished Greeks caged in dark walls." The barbarian Ingomar is the real free man, passing the days in the thick bush and scaling the mountain passes. He urges her to be his bride and to adopt the ways of his people. Parthenia responds sadly that she cannot forsake her aged parents nor renounce the worship of her gods. After some hesitation a disconsolate Ingomar proclaims "then so will I leave my nation, manners, all to follow thee. I will become a Greek."

At the city walls the pair encounter her father who embraces Parthenia joyfully. But despite her reassurances that the barbarian chieftain seeks only Greek citizenship, the father regards Ingomar with suspicion. As a test of his sincerity, the armorer requests him to replace his skin garment with the Greek dress, to cut short his hair and beard, and to surrender his sword. In addition, he must agree to work in the fields and vineyards and to toil with plow and harrow. While Ingomar protests haughtily that such labors insult "my proud race's mark of free descent," the sight of a smiling Parthenia dissolves all hesitation.

The fifth and final act opens with a moment of trial. The sudden appearance of the Alemanni band arouses apprehension among the Greek inhabitants. Polydor (supported by an Actea ever hopeful that her daughter would yet marry him) charges that "Ingomar is a spy and traitor in conspiracy with the Alemanni to pillage Massilia." Parthenia reproaches her mother for spreading such a malicious rumor. She records the noble deeds of Ingomar since he had become a Greek. He had destroyed "the wolf that had so long ravaged our fields, . . . sprung to the rescue of Lysippus when his boat struggled with the storm, . . . and who but he relieves from the forge and the plough my gray-haired father."

More shrewdly, the Timarch hopes to turn the presence of Ingomar to advantage in the defense of the city. He dangles before him full-citizen privileges and a house, three hides of land, and thirty ounces of silver as the dower of Parthenia in the event of their marriage. On his part Ingomar must go to the camp of the Alemanni "as though thou camest to seek thy friends and hear the news of home." But his real mission would be to observe the approaches to their camp, discover their watchword, and note the arrangements for security. Then, after returning to the city, on that same night, Ingomar must conduct Massilia's soldiers to an easy conquest of the Alemanni.

Ingomar reacts furiously, crying out: "Ensnare, betray my countrymen! Deceive the men who trust me—murder them in their sleep—the men who speak my tongue, who were my brothers?" Had he been called on to fight for Massilia on the open field of battle, he would have stood faithfully by the city to the death. An equally furious Timarch bades Ingomar to hold his tongue and gives him one hour for decision and if negative "thence no longer contaminate our city." A despairing Ingomar laments the fact that now Parthenia will be lost to him forever. But to his astonishment and joy Parthenia approaches with his sword and tells him that she will bear it for him wherever his wandering steps might lead them. More than this, she confesses that for long she has loved him but kept the secret locked in her heart.

A new element of conflict is introduced by Polydor who announces that he has bought up the debts of Myron from his creditors. According to Greek law he demands the personages of Parthenia and her parents as slaves. Ingomar offers himself as a slave in their place and a reluctant Polydor accepts the substitution lest he be physically set upon. At that doleful moment the Alemanni band advance upon the city and seek out Ingomar. Their mission, as they explain to the Timarch, is to reassure themselves that Ingomar remains a free man in his new environment. A quaking Timarch, fearful for the survival of Massilia, accompanies them to the home of Myron. There Ingomar responds frankly that he has indeed just become a slave, albeit of his own volition, and points to Polydor as the responsible culprit. Not until the Timarch agrees to pay the ransom to Polydor does Ingomar feel that his pledge has been kept and that his erstwhile countrymen can go on their way at rest as to the status of their former chieftain.

But surprises are still in store for all concerned. The Timarch has second thoughts to the effect that perhaps a more positive policy towards the Alemanni might be desirable. First, he orders attendants to drive forth beyond the city walls the wretched Polydor for the peril to which his greed had exposed Massilia. Second, he would assign territory to the Alemanni to form a colony of which Ingomar would be the Timarch. Needless to say, Ingomar accepts with joy and embraces Parthenia. Together they recite the true nature of love: "Two souls with but a single thought, Two hearts that beat as one."

Critiques

What sort of critique can be assembled as a basis for further evaluating the potential attributes of *Ingomar* in terms of social significance? William Winter, a seasoned New York dramatic critic and author of books about the stage, was a staunch defender of the play. He scoffed at those devotees of "theatrical pepper" who regarded *Ingomar* as somewhat "archaic and insipid." Cynicism might sneer at its impossible story and at such blind allegiance to classicism but:

> "our Theatre [1913] sadly needs relief from a burdensome destructive literature of vice and folly, and until superior modern talent provides a dramatic fabric in which equal purity of spirit, romance of atmosphere, and beauty of feeling are displayed in a better way, and in accordance with prosaic probability, *Ingomar* ought always to receive a cordial welcome."

What the playwright had achieved was a delicate texture of poetic fancy completely elusive of the test of fact but suffused with the pervasion of nobility. The allegory was one that should impart cheer and encouragement to every believer in the possible goodness of human nature and in the attainment of a little felicity in human affections. The theme trumpeted the conquest of arrogant strength by gentleness, of ignorance by knowledge, of brutality by refinement, of barbaric passion by perfect innocence, of animal lust by spiritual resurrection.

As Winter interpreted the role of Parthenia, the Greek girl must impart to the barbarians the decisive impression of courage and honor. She must accept the effect of unconscious capability of heroism and artless candor as well as the epitome of absolute innocence and simplicity. The gradual growth of Parthenia's awareness of her subjugation of the barbarian chief and of her own subjugation must be deftly and subtly depicted. The part called for a girl possessed of warmth, loveliness, and the glamor of spontaneous virtue, all flowing from a liberated spirit. To put it another way, there must be "a sweet, genuine, winning individuality in the performer and the consistent maintenance of a condition of feminine enticement and at once piquant and demure," seemingly conflicting frames of behavior that would require a dramatic effort of the utmost sensitivity. It would be interesting to know whether these feminine qualities were actually supplied by the author in the given circumstances of the play or nuances an actress created and translated into her personality. In any event, presumably Winter would argue that *Ingomar* met the essence of a classical plot in its emphasis upon purity of taste, sobriety, dignity, and formal elegance. Among the audience, if the message of human refinement was to reach its mark, the performance should evoke a sense of conscious nobility and spiritual wholesomeness.

A source for the cordial reception which *Ingomar* received on the west coast is McMinn's *The Theater of the Golden Era in California* (1941). He referred to a review in a San Francisco journal called the *Golden Era* (1855) which impressed the author as evidence that sophisticated critics were not lacking on the Pacific coast. It dwelt at length upon the particular performance of Jean Davenport, the latest Parthenia to appear on the California stage. She did not seem to have realized the romantic charm and warmth and tenderness of the Grecian maid as most surely was intended to be drawn. Her voice was wanting in modulation and inexpressive of forlorn pathos and deep feeling. The professional actress was certainly always present but the soul that ought to inspire every gesture and utterance did not gleam through. Compared with Mrs. Stark, "the best representative of Parthenia upon our boards," Jean Davenport fell short of the desirable standard. But in the way of sentimental romance *Ingomar* did meet all the primary requirements of a classical plot, notwithstanding the performance of any particular individual.

McMinn referred also to a review in the *San Francisco Evening Bulletin* "as late as 1856, long after this play had established itself as a favorite."

After providing readers with a fairly-detailed synopsis of the play, the critic went on to discuss its merits. The theme of the triumph of natural goodness over civilized baseness and of a noble savage's superiority over the false aristocrat in standards of conduct still made for popular drama. But despite the male emphasis in the title of the play, it was Parthenia who stood forth as the principal character. Perhaps an Ingomar who postured and stormed could force himself upon an audience with his demonstration of manly virility. Yet it was Parthenia who won the acclaim of the audience with her lovely artlessness by which she subdued her volcanic lover and had him soon collecting a maiden's flowers and bearing the basket of plucked berries.

What, apart from entertainment, could have been the derivative benefits of *Ingomar* for transforming a hardy group of pioneers into a civilized community? More specifically, it may well be inquired what a frontier settlement such as Humboldt County was then could find invigorating and ennobling in this drama. Whether the locale be the expanse of a forest primeval in southern France or the walls of a Greek city, a sense of dignified loyalty carried the assurance of community stability. Even the Alemanni, however much they might live by the sword, had a code of honorable conduct. They were prepared to accept the departure of Ingomar from their ranks upon the knowledge of his status as a free man in Greek society. Nor would Ingomar permit himself to be less than a man of chivalry and turn upon his kinsfolk in the guise of a spy or a traitor. On his part the Timarch came to recognize the manliness of Ingomar in disdaining an unworthy strategem to gain a victory. In the end the Timarch extended neighborliness to the Alemanni, perhaps even appreciating the possibilities of cultural mingling for a peaceful world.

Nor could there be an audience unawareness of the filial responsibilities inherent in the family system. To be sure, Actea leaves something to be desired as a mother concerned for the happiness of her daughter. It was unworthy of her to berate Parthenia as a "selfish and ungrateful child" for refusing Polydor and so dooming her parents to poverty in their old age. Then, too, during the confrontation between the Timarch and Ingomar, the conduct of Myron was not above reproach. Warned by the Timarch that he would answer with his life if "thou dost befriend or shelter him," the armorer strained the milk of human gratitude in his cringing reaction. For the ears of the Timarch he shouted that "I will have nothing more to do with him, away, depart, . . . I shut my door against thee."

Yet, despite such trials of family perversity, Parthenia manifested a high degree of filial devotion. She was concerned over the arduous toil wearing down her aged parents and vowed to end her own playful ways. She would become a model of industrious application to domestic chores. What could be more demonstrative than the decision to surrender herself to the Alemanni as a hostage in place of her enslaved father. No less poignant was the emotional scene when Ingomar returned Parthenia to the embrace of her father. Indeed, the depth of the solicitude nourished by the many hours spent at the family hearth was never better illustrated than by her willingness to wed the unprepossessing Polydor in order to save her debt-ridden parents from the abyss of slavery. Only the burden shouldered by Ingomar to claim captivity for himself prevented the sacrifice of her womanhood.

Most exemplary was the glorification of a mature love as the bond for a true marriage. From the very outset Parthenia countered parental pressure for a union of pecuniary advantage with the recollection that the songs of childhood spoke always of the heart. Love must enter unsought and grow until it burst every restraining force and broke upon the startled soul with a paean of joy. As a hostage in the forest she explained to Ingomar that in the Greek community "we consult our hearts... bound by choice with bands as light sweet as the garlands she held." But she confessed that she herself had not yet felt any stirring. On the other hand, Ingomar seemed to have caught the virus quickly, forsaking the chase, lolling on the grass, and listening to her songs and tales. Unhappily, on one occasion, before he could discipline his headiness, he grasped her hands roughly. Thereupon, Parthenia reacted apprehensively and drew a dagger to her breast and Ingomar desisted. She admonished him, stressing the theme that love is a mystic dream and not a thing of forwardness, a pulsating of rapture and not a thing to blast and to scorch. After all, her own name was a symbol of maidenly virginity, memorialized on the Acropolis at Athens by the sacred temple of Parthenon.

The courtship had to weather still further crises before a decorous comradeship prevailed. A proud Ingomar did not take kindly to the everlasting homilies of Parthenia. He boasted of noble rank won by resounding feats of war. Parthenia responded spiritedly that she was Massilia's freeborn daughter, "nourished on a pure mother's breast, cradled in the arms of beauty and refinement, reared from childhood in the holy service of our righteous gods." This bitter exchange went so far as to witness a proud Ingomar brandishing his sword and shouting that "thy sight is poison." In the end he found the prospect of separation from Parthenia too bleak a future and agreed to settle in Massilia. If Parthenia strove to make the transition a comforting one, she withheld any outward manifestation of her inward warmth. It required the ultimatum of the Timarch that Ingomar be cast out of the city for Parthenia to declare openly her love. As they embraced she confessed humbly:

> "that long have I been thine. Ay since the day when thou didst learn to weep and fear, when from thy hand dropped the uplifted sword which

threatened at my life. If in shame I tried to hide it from thee, I only loved thee more."

Whatever merit there might be in speculative thoughts, it would be interesting to know how local citizens interpreted the play. Certainly the contents of Monroe's dedicatory speech inferred exchanges of views among concerned Eurekans for the state of theatrical offerings. He had made every effort to impress upon patrons that their support to match the adventurous spirit of Carson was vital to make of the stage a cultural experience. Even the attraction of being just entertained need not be discounted if on a higher level than most of the current forms of amusement. At any rate, a discriminating leadership could promote plays like *Ingomar*, illustrating the lessons of wisdom and truth, the love of beauty and goodness, the purity and elegance of the English language, the refinement of public taste and manners, and the mystery of the soul. To which one might add that perhaps the analogy of *Ingomar* contrasting a primitive life with a more sedentary and sophisticated community suggested the relationship between an emergent Eureka and the metropolis of San Francisco to the south. For William Carson, well-conversed with its plot and inspirational message, a frontier community could assuredly do no better than follow its precepts in seeking identification with American civilization at its best.

CHAPTER SEVEN

INGOMAR THEATRE: A NARRATIVE

Local Scene

ANY HISTORY OF THE Ingomar Theatre (and Carson Mansion) should furnish some account of the local scene by the eighteen-nineties. Ethel E. Bangert in her article in the *California Highway Patrolman* (March 1950, p. 22) would introduce the subject by describing Eureka as a town known by its superlatives: "the *westernmost* city of the United States; the one with the most *outstanding* Victorian house; the place with the *highest* Christmas tree; near the *only whaling* station on the continent." And for past decades, if the writer had been aware of it, she could have included "the loveliest playhouse between San Francisco and Portland." For such information as follows, a number of sources were relied upon and may be listed: 1) *History of Humboldt County* (1882), Wallace W. Elliott, publisher; 2) Hamm, *History and Business Directory of Humboldt County* (1890); 3) *Humboldt County Souvenir* (1904, 2nd ed.); 4) Irvine, *History of Humboldt County* (1915); 5) Eddy, J. M., compiler, *In the Redwood's Realm* (1893); 6) *Humboldt Historian, 1953-present* (includes the *Newsletter*).

In terms of population Humboldt County had shown a steady increase: 15,500 (1880); 23,500 (1890); 27,000 (1900); and today hovers about 100,000. Besides Eureka the better known communities included Alton, Arcata, Blue Lake, Bucksport, Ferndale, Fortuna, Hydesville, Loleta, Rohnerville, and Scotia. The economy was varied and in most instances for domestic consumption and self-sufficiency. Dairy farms not only supplied the local demand for milk but also set up creameries for butter production. The availability of grazing land enabled the raising of cattle to supply the demand for meat. An offshoot was the establishment of several tanneries for leather production. Some farmers stocked sheep, offering mutton and wool to the local communities. Fishing was excellent, especially salmon, and fish canneries began to operate. The equable climate and ample rainfall (an annual average of some forty inches) encouraged horticulture and farming. The orchards yielded apples, peaches, plums, prunes, pears, and cherries. In the way of berries the most successful were strawberries, raspberries, and currants. Apart from what the farms bottled as preserves, jellies, and jams, there were fruit canneries catering to the town trade. Nurseries sprang up to fill the demands for trees, plants, and landscaping. The cultivation of the soil stressed the production of oats, potatoes, barley, wheat, and Indian corn. The principal mining centered about granite quarries although some gold was found. Facilities were developed to provide iron, brick, and tile. For the rest, Humboldt County could claim to be a sportsman's paradise, boasting such outdoor activities as boating, hunting, fishing, and beaches. Nor ought the fact be overlooked that the many sheltered hillsides and valleys provided a playground for family picnics, reached by steamer schooner, horse and buggy, and local railroads.

Eureka had emerged as the metropolis of northern California, wresting that role from Bucksport to the south and Arcata to the north. Since 1856 it had served as the county seat. In terms of population it had likewise shown a steady increase: 3,500 (1880); 7,000 (1890); 10,000 (1900); and today hovers about 25,000. As the terminus of the several railroad lines operating in the county, it was favorably situated to become the distribution center for supplies. Until the railroad line to San Francisco became a reality in 1914, the principal means of transcontinental travel was the semi-weekly steamer carrying mail, bulk, and passengers to its port. But the uncertainty of vessels getting across the sand bar was a constant nightmare. A delay of days going or coming was always a possibility and preyed upon the minds of captains, crews, and passengers. Travel overland by stage from San Francisco was slower, the distance close to 300 miles, and usually took several days although it could be done in good weather by express in two days. That the trip presented an adventure might be inferred from a local item in the *Times-Telephone* (June 26, 1883) to the effect that John Dolbeer and party were elated with their achievement by private conveyance. In comparison, the distance by ship was about 220 nautical miles and the estimated time of passage ranged from 17 to 27 hours. Needless to say, the waterfront portrayed a busy scene of vessels arriving and departing. The local newspaper columns reflected this fact, carrying the scheduled lists of passengers and the destinations of the lumber schooners.

The economic base of Eureka rested largely on the presence of sawmills and shipbuilding yards. The logging companies floated the felled trees from the nearby timber reserves down the tidewater or conveyed them via the railroads to the local wharves where the sawmills were located. The shipyards, notably the H. D. Bendixsen Ways (Gibbs, *West Coast Windjammers*, 1968, pp. 45-50), had by the eighteen-nineties turned out over 150 coastal and off-shore craft including some of the schooners owned by the Dolbeer and Carson Lumber Company. The chief asset was the harbor in Humboldt Bay, described as second only to San Francisco in northern California. The bay was listed as fourteen miles in length with a varying width from one-half to four miles and superior in water depth to Arcata on the northern shore. But for long the chief drawback had been the sand bar. After much public agitation and political pressure the federal government undertook a series of improvements. Between 1887 and 1894 the channel was dredged and rock jetties constructed at a cost of over $2,000,000, making the harbor more accessible and to larger vessels. To acquaint the nation with the endless opportunities in the community a chamber of commerce had been founded in 1883.

City blocks in Eureka were square and the streets at right angles to each other. By this time the reader should be aware that the main thoroughfares were identified by the letters of the alphabet and arabic numbers, a practice common in the towns of the county. The sidewalks were wooden and the roads graveled although future plans called for "macadamization." At night the streets were illuminated by the lights posted on masts and merchants were delighted by the opportunity to keep their stores open in the evening. In this connection, the frequent references to specific business addresses are to remind inhabitants of past landmarks. For local transportation there were in 1888 three miles of tracks, six cars with the power supplied by a complement of twenty-five horses, and the fare was five cents. The count of daily passengers amounted to about 700. But the system went out of existence in 1897 due to financial losses. In 1903 it was replaced by electric cars purchased secondhand. On the first day of operation over 3,000 passengers paid fares and "many more rode on the car steps where the conductor could not reach them." The amenities for a comfortable material existence were not lacking. Both telegraph and telephone facilities for rapid communication were being made available. In fact, the extension of the telegraph to Eureka in 1874 had prompted the *Weekly Humboldt Times* on January 3 to announce the addition of a daily newspaper. The water system was described as excellent, supplying pure water from the Elk River five miles from the city limits. The fire department was staffed partly by salaried personnel and supplemented with volunteers. The financial needs were provided by five commercial banks and two savings institutions.

The cultural opportunities of the city were not entirely meager. There were two daily and four weekly newspapers besides a steady trickle of hopeful but short-lived ones in circulation. More than a dozen churches offered spiritual guidance to the citizenry while a score of social and charitable societies were available to channel the recreational and humanitarian impulses along worthwhile paths. A public school system provided primary and secondary courses of study. In addition, at times there would seem to have been private educational ventures, notably a girls' academy and a business or secretarial institute. Incidentally, the Carson boys were sent to preparatory schools in the San Francisco Bay area, as were most children of the wealthy. A steady expansion of library holdings is to be recorded, progressing from a membership association charging fees to a free public library. The latter eventually acquired its own building, financed by a grant of $20,000 from the Carnegie Foundation plus $10,000 raised by contributions from public-spirited citizens. One may well feel confident that William Carson was among the generous donors.

In short, Eureka had acquired by the closing decades of the nineteenth century the symbols of a dynamic and progressive town. But it should not be supposed that it was without human problems to challenge the vision of a civilized community. To many it was known as a flamboyant town overrun with boisterous sailors and rough-and-tumble lumberjacks, cheap hotels, waterfront saloons, and camp followers of easy virtue. The columns of the newspapers were replete with accounts of clashes between the white settlers and the American Indians over land claims. Equally in the headlines was the issue of the competition between white labor and the Chinese as well as the difficulties attendant upon the assimilation of the latter. In the way of moral deficiencies, the presence of drunkenness and prostitution, the never-ending gunplay and knifings, and the shoddy hovels on the other side of the "railroad tracks" were matters of social concern. Nor was nature always beneficent, for fires and floods were a constant threat and when unleashed played havoc with lives and property. Verily, the west as the utopia of the future had its work cut out to strengthen the quality of human dignity and to cope with the natural elements.

Ingomar Performances

This is not to say that concerned citizens regarded the playhouse as the answer to the tribulations of the community. Rather it could constitute one possible approach for a society seeking a meaningful stability. For the overall history of the Ingomar Theatre a convenient reference is an unpublished master's thesis completed at the University of California, Los

Angeles, by Frank Bernard Bettendorf entitled, *Dramatic Activities of the Humboldt Bay Area, 1880-1912* (1963). For the immediate years the theater was certainly kept busy, as the chart of Bettendorf shows. The central fact was the presence of several traveling companies, from three to six annually, for engagements of about a week, each with varied repertories. The belief of some present-day local historians that townspeople were often used by economy-minded professional companies for nominal appearances on the stage or as backstage voices or to fill gaps in choruses is not backed by documentary evidence. Neither Bettendorf's study nor accounts in Eurekan newspapers of performances contains any references along this line. In addition, the theater was available for concerts, musicals, and amateur performances. But according to the *Fountain Papers* (volume 64, p. 262) the theater was never used on Sundays as the Carsons were very pious and their sons followed the custom which must have been a costly ban. The compiler of this source continues that "the only concession the Carsons ever made on Sunday exhibitions was when a local church wanted to put on a presentation of some kind and they were granted the use of the house for free, of course."

A pertinent topic is the frequency of the performance of *Ingomar*, the virtues of which had prompted Carson to see in the theater an agency for good. It was not until April 1895 that a professional company appeared which included in its repertory a vehicle so popular among leading actors and actresses and drew large audiences. The Rose Stillman company had been playing in San Francisco and agreed to come for a week's engagement. From April 14 on, the local newspapers provided a running commentary on the daily performances and the size of audiences. Manager Wells was commended for wisely reducing prices to get good crowds, the tariff ranging from 25 cents to 50 cents. It was hoped that "our local 400 will no doubt be out in full force" to set an example. Despite inclement weather the audiences were described as from fair-sized to excellent for the melange of plays—*The Parisian Princess, That Precious Baby, The Noble Outcast, Man and Master, The Clemenceau Case,* and *East Lynne.*

Ingomar was reserved for Saturday, April 20, the *Standard* feeling it necessary to recall for readers "it is from this play that the Ingomar Theatre was named but, strange to say, the play has never been put on at the above-named house . . . and special costumes have been secured for the occasion." The *Times* (April 20) likewise made the point that it is "the first production at this theatre of the drama from which the house was named; although rather late for the baptismal performance, it will lose nothing by it" as the company had made a special effort to hold rehearsals.

Both local newspapers provided reviews of the *Ingomar* production. The *Times* (April 21) placed its seal of approval upon the presentation:

> "*Ingomar* gave the company an opportunity to show their ability in other lines than those of comedy and melodrama. Fremont and Rose Stillman showed a fine conception of the characters and although the play was new to many, their efforts were thoroughly appreciated. As Actea, Miss Hattie Foley, as usual, was painstaking in her portrayal, while Harold Vizard as Polydor in makeup and characterization was a surprise."

The *Standard* (April 22) noted a much larger audience than on previous nights but nothing in proportion to what the attraction deserved. In any event, although the critique must have left readers in doubt as to the message to be derived, "it was the best performance of the whole week [and] the audience was well pleased." Miss Stillman took the role of Parthenia and A. W. Fremont displayed a "fine voice and handsome stage presence" as Ingomar.

The next recorded presentation of *Ingomar* transpired on January 16, 1899, the opening production of the Janet Waldorf company. The review in the *Standard* (January 17) applauded the performance as thoroughly first-class. While the play had been given here "many times [!], both by amateurs and professionals, the consensus of opinion expressed among the audience was that such a superb production had never before been put on in Eureka." Indeed, the occasion prompted an enthusiastic editor to congratulate the manager for bringing these talented performers to town. Whether or not a return to standard ticket prices—dress circle ($1.00), orchestra (75 cents), gallery (50 to 25 cents)—had reduced attendance, it was to be regretted that only a "fair-sized audience was attracted, for the play was worthy of a full house." However, local cultural leaders were encouraged by the increasing attendance on succeeding nights for the plays that followed, including *Twelfth Night, As You Like It, Romeo and Juliet,* and *The Hunchback,* a heady diet rarely repeated by succeeding companies. The semi-weekly issue of the *Standard* (January 25, 1899) carried the news that theater parties were organized from Fortuna, Loleta, and Arcata, traveling in specially-chartered excursion trains.

Local newspapers did not ignore this time the equally vital cultural task of providing their readers with a critique of the *Ingomar* performance. On the eve of the presentation the *Times* (January 14, 1899) quoted the appraisal of an unidentified eastern newspaper with regard to the Parthenia role played by Janet Waldorf:

> "Miss Waldorf's face is her fortune, not that it is so beautiful, but because it is so rich in expression. Every changing mood, every sweep of passion, is mirrored in her countenance, and before a word is uttered, the auditor knows well what his heroine is about to say. She could act her part and never speak a line. With this face nature has

given her a voice of wondrous range and richness, modulated to a sweetness not given to one woman in a thousand and her every movement is grace itself."

Subsequently, on January 17, the *Times* rendered its judgment on the *Ingomar* production which the Eurekans themselves attended:

> "The press reports which have heralded the company's appearance, although flattering, contained no meed of praise that was not deserved.
> Miss Janet Waldorf is a talented young woman of more than prepossessing appearance, and her acting shows her to be not only talented, but versatile as well. Her facial expression is marvellous, and if she did not read a line, the auditor could clearly interpret the meaning she intends to convey.
> Mr. William McVey, the leading man, as Ingomar sustained his part in a highly creditable manner. He is possessed of a fine face, physique, and voice, and made a noble and realistic barbarian chief.
> Mr. Norval McGregor, in the character of Polydor, a merchant, was well up in his part, and the rest of the cast carried their parts in fine manner."

The *Standard* (January 17, 1899) was no less fulsome in its praise. If Miss Waldorf had youth, beauty, and grace, she gave ample evidence of careful and unremitting study. Through the powerful "alembic [distilling] of her own personality, she became a revivified Parthenia speaking the lines of the heroine but withal a winsome, charming entity all her own." Her love scenes were tender and her tragedies sublime. William McVey made a magnificent Ingomar, "a man of thews and sinews," with a deep and profound voice "that quells the snarling of his barbarian horde and mellows . . . by the power of love." The balance of the cast was well sustained and the play was adequately costumed and staged. One might have wished that these several reviews had taken in hand the question of the play's civilizing attributes and counselled the local audience on the lessons to be taken to heart in the way of a design for refined living.

So pleased were the local theatergoers with the Janet Waldorf company that Manager Wells contracted for another engagement (March 16-18, 1899), persuading them to break their itinerary from a schedule that would take the troupe from San Francisco to Seattle and thence on to the Orient with stops at Honolulu and Manila. Two new plays would be presented— *Lady of Lyons* and *Much Ado About Nothing*. Originally a Saturday matinee was planned with a mixed bill of the third act of *Ingomar* (its flower scene was deemed the most popular) and *Pygmalion and Galatea*. A vote was taken among the devotees of the stage and the decision was to do *Ingomar* in its entirety at the matinee and to present *Camille* for the evening performance. Apparently *Ingomar* was put on especially for school children and tickets were distributed to schools, to be exchanged at the box office for a regular ticket at 25 cents to all parts of the house with a price of 50 cents for the ladies. The *Standard* (March 18) reported that the attendance was "the largest for any similar occasion for many a day." It was an appreciative audience and a fine production. The *Times* (March 21) added its approval to what seemed a concerted effort to nurture an enthusiasm among the younger generation for the legitimate theater.

The daily *Standard* and its semi-weekly issue provided space for interesting vignettes about the brief engagement. It was marvelous to have brought them back for a second engagement in such a short time and to have them draw attendances breaking the record of previous companies with wider intervals of visits. They had succeeded on merit alone. The unusual demand for seats from outside towns was noted, even from so remote a place as Blocksburg in the southern corner of Humboldt County. Every mail brought orders for seats from the valley towns. To satisfy the demand from the north the management arranged for an excursion from Blue Lake and intervening towns along the line of the Arcata and Mad River Railroad. The train would leave Arcata at 7 P.M. and return immediately after the performance, the fare being one dollar for the round trip and included the price of a reserved seat in the theater. But it was distressing to hear the complaints against "a certain band of calves" who had made themselves obnoxious in the gallery. It was understood that the house employed a special policeman whose duty required him to keep order but either his authority had not been exhibited or it was not recognized.

Subsequent History

The euphoria generated by the second visit of the Janet Waldorf company was not lost upon Manager Wells. The *Standard* (March 20, 1899) reported him as announcing a good line-up for the months ahead of comedy, drama, and opera (operettas). Bettendorf is rather dubious, however, of the long-term effect. The number of imported companies performing serious drama during the span he examined to the year 1912 seemed relatively few. Nor did he think audience interest in attendance at the theater was sustained. He attributed the dilemma partly to the fact that the schedule did not include plays of Ibsen, Strindberg, and Chekhov (to which might be added Shaw) whose themes were more in the mainstream of changing social *mores*. Certainly, elsewhere in the nation, there was an abrupt slackening in the productions of *Ingomar*, practically disappearing from repertories after World War I. Part of the dilemma would seem to have been the increasing trend of local critics to extol the desire of people for laughter and entertainment. In defense of the local newspapers, if their dramatic critiques were not apt to make the public keen students of what theatricals strove to accomplish, it should be remembered that editors could not be experts in all fields.

An interesting glimpse of how the Ingomar Theatre fitted into the life of the community may be had from an article in the *Times* (March 2, 1941) written by Marie Croghan (Conry) Jones, the society editor. She recalled to a new generation the playhouse and the glories that had been as she remembered them. The occasion was the discovery of a number of programs and leaflets of past performances, dug up by electricians of the utility company while working under the F Street stairway entrance. She put the seating capacity at 1,164 but still a very cozy and intimate theater with perfect acoustics. The boxes were richly decorated and the thickly-piled carpets were the last word in luxury. Heavy golden drapes of Irish linen in rich folds divided the dress circle under the extended gallery from the orchestra pit. Unless the reference is to loops around the brass railings, it seems at variance with the color scheme of electric blue throughout the interior. The presentations included vocalists, violinists, operettas, amateur dramas, and minstrel shows. Such noted singers as Mme. Schumann-Heink and Mackenzie Gordon appeared on the immense stage. Very vivid still was the story of Mrs. General Tom Thumb in January 1893, detained for an interminable time by the vicissitudes of the Humboldt bar and compounded by *mal de mer*. An Eurekan visitor to Paris in 1908 reminded the lady in question of this episode and Mrs. General Tom Thumb's reputed response was akin to a nightmare. Nevertheless, in retrospect, the memories were many and rich about this "gem of theatres."

Still, despite the growing minimal role of the only playhouse in Eureka that remained true to the stage as an effective civilizing influence, Carson maintained the structure in good repair. In 1896, for example, he posted automatic sprinklers by the stage and in the dressing rooms, scenery wing, and engine shop. Even more extensive were fire precaution arrangements in October 1904 in the wake of the Iroquois Theatre holocaust in Chicago which took the lives of several hundred people. Carson had never been satisfied with the dispersal of the audience, for there was always the danger of a panic as the spectators streaming from the gallery jostled with those emerging from the main floor at the head of the stairs leading down to the exits. The new plan called for cutting into the wall at the back of the gallery between the upper landings of the two stairways. From the wide opening thus cleared a broad stairway would be obtained leading down into the rear room of one of the suites. In this way the crowd would come together in the spacious corridor at the lower level outside the theater portion where a more rapid emptying of the premises was possible. Behind the private boxes the steps would be replaced by inclined floors as a safety measure. From the dress circle the back two rows would be removed, allowing more room for passage out. In addition, metal fire escapes were to be installed on the alley side of the building as an alternate exit for patrons from both gallery and main floor in the event of dense smoke and fire inside blocking the regular passageways.

At the same time plans were also made to renovate the furnishings after more than a decade of wear and tear. The carpets at the entrance to the lower corridor were replaced, the former with cork matting and the latter with rubber cloth. The carpets in the foyer and the aisles were taken up and cleaned and relaid. Ceilings and walls were replastered where necessary, kalsomined, and frescoed over. The *Standard* (October 15, 1904) commended the alterations, observing happily "that the pretty little playhouse which was always neat in appearance now looks like new." Not to be outdone the *Times* (October 16, 1904) noted that "within a short time it will in truth be the neatest, safest, and most convenient upper story theatre on the coast."

The immediate aftermath revealed a resumption of scheduled activities. In the *Fountain Papers* (volume 64, p. 269) a note, dated December 1, 1906, recorded that:

> "Manager Wells who returned from a trip to San Francisco Monday made arrangements for the best stock company on the coast to play a week's engagement each month at the local playhouse. The talent secured is the Colonial Stock Company from the Colonial Theatre, now the leading theatre in the city."

But Bettendorf insists that the use of the theater for dramatic efforts lessened and the audiences for such performances grew smaller and smaller. Occasionally traveling companies would present two shows and then leave town. Indeed, for periods at a time the playhouse remained inactive. Nor did the behavior of spectators improve, for there were frequent statements in the newspapers of unruly conduct. To add to the disillusionment an assorted list of events were scheduled—hypnotist, recitals, guest lecturers, school graduation exercises, war bond sales, memorial services of the Elks Lodge. And the future boded ill with the appearance of the Theatre Margarita as a rival playhouse. It was the old E Street Theatre, remodeled and renamed for Margarita Fischer who played most of the leads in the productions. Then, too, stock companies were brought in by her and one actress, Marjorie Rambeau, later to become a star on Broadway and in the movies, received her apprenticeship in this manner (as did Donald Crisp and Paul Harvey).

The result was a growing reliance once more upon amateur dramatic societies but even these found the only means of playing before full houses was to put on musicals, comedies, farces, and melodrama. Then there was the competition of vaudeville and movies with their cheaper prices— evenings 15, 25, and 35 cents and matinees 10 and 20 cents. Even the Theatre Margarita found the going rough, running into financial difficulties, changing ownership, and turning to "humorous and instructive movies." Part of the dilemma would seem still to have been the trend among local reviewers to be critical of serious drama and to prefer extolling the desire of the public for laughter and entertainment. In any event, the era of the frontier west had passed and Eureka moved into the twentieth century and to the challenge of new generations. Whether the Ingomar Theatre had served a constructive purpose in its time is one of those intangibles ever susceptible to speculations.

Finally, on December 25, 1923, the *Standard* carried the story that John Milton had decided to close the theater permanently. He felt that it was costing too much money to maintain the Ingomar Theatre considering its lack of usage. The announced sale of the upholstered opera chairs meant the dismantling of a cultural landmark which for more than three decades had provided a worthy home for stage plays. It would be interesting to know whether the theater had ever been financially self-sustaining. More likely it had entailed annual losses even in the lifetime of Carson. If it will be recalled, Alonzo Judson Monroe in his dedicatory speech (*Times*, December 23, 1892) hinted at that fact in his observation "it is apparent when we consider that the building of this theatre is not a mere business proposition [but] a contribution from a public-spirited citizen to his fellow citizens." To which might be affixed the comment in the *Standard* (November 12, 1892) apropos its vote of thanks to Carson for the newly-built theater "that it can hardly be a very remunerative investment [let alone the time and worry its management and safety provisions must have involved]." In the *Fountain Papers* (volume 64, p. 262) there is an unidentified newspaper clipping (sometime after 1923) which makes the same point in the colorful vernacular "that one venture of Carson was a dud financially. . . . the Ingomar Theatre that never made a dime for [him] or anyone else." But, assuredly, Carson would not have minded the losses any more than he did the annual deficits in his affiliated church which he helped to make up if his cultural adventure had shared in preparing Eureka for a civilized role.

To complete the history of the Ingomar Theatre, the entire building was sold shortly to the Buhne Hardware company which used the interior of the playhouse as a store room for baling wire, kegs of nails, and tar paper. Then, in 1958, it was again sold and leased to a furniture mart which planned to remodel the inside for sales rooms. The new owner agreed to allow the Humboldt County Historical Society to sponsor for a week what was termed "The Final Curtain Call." Both local newspapers carried a daily commentary on the events which were held from Tuesday, April 8 through Sunday, April 13, 1 to 5 P.M. To defray expenses, although many volunteered their services free, an admission fee of 50 cents for adults and 25 cents for young people was charged. Souvenir programs were also sold. Asta Culberg, active in local historical circles, in a paper read before the *Conference of California Historical Societies* (volume V, No. 3, September 1958, pp. 304-305), held on the Stockton campus of the College of the Pacific, provided the statistics for the successful event. Some 3,000 copies of the souvenir program were printed and sold. The total receipts came to $1,322.30. The total expenses, including the cost of fire insurance to cover the days of the open house and the presence of firemen at all hours the public trooped through, came to $261.90, leaving a net profit of $1,060.40. But more than this, it had awakened interest in local history and fostered a determination to preserve whatever remained of a rich heritage.

Certainly, the three thousand visitors were treated to an interesting program. They were taken on tours and shown the architectural, historical, and theatrical highlights. Lectures were scheduled and even taped to acquaint the rising generation with the wonders of the past. For the elderly the historical sketch presented by Mrs. Stanley Roscoe must have recalled many nostalgic moments. Performances were given by the Pistol River State Teachers College, the Dixieland Band, the Eureka High School Band, and the Sweet Adelines. One gentleman whose appearances on the Ingomar stage dated back fifty years offered a segment of his role in the Gilbert and Sullivan operetta *H.M.S. Pinafore*. A collection of old-time photo slides and the original blueprints of the building were put on display. An amateur camera contest was held bearing a prize of ten dollars, the subject to be the interior of the theater. A precious by-product was the accumulation of many valuable photo duplicates from the contestants. On the last day, Sunday, April 13, at 5 P.M., as the three blinks on the carbon-filamented electric lights announced the end of a saga, those present sang "Auld Lang Syne," accompanied no doubt by many a tear trickling down cheeks. Bettendorf includes at the back of his thesis a number of photographs taken of the theater as visitors were being guided through its stilled hall. And for a postscript mention might be made of a program issued by the women's organization of the Christ Episcopal Church, dated November 18, 1965, entitled *Eureka That Was*. It includes a sketch of the theater's interior and the accompanying necrology, *1892-1958*.

That a rich segment of the historical past is in danger of complete obliteration is evident to the writer. Not many Eurekans can readily answer inquiries on the subject of the Ingomar Theatre and many more profess ignorance of its whereabouts. There is no outward sign that it had been the Carson Block. It has been stuccoed and the original brick facade remains only on the alley side. The shabby-looking bay windows on the upper stories alone are a reassurance of the structure's identity. The lovely arches at the F Street entrance have been stuccoed over to establish straight lines. The windows and entrances on the alley side are either boarded up or the victims of concrete slabs. Frank Simas, the tenant of the furniture mart which occupies the building and uses the theater portion still as a warehouse, was gracious enough to volunteer as a guide. He pointed out at the cashier's counter the marble top once used for the box office. There are false ceilings and lowered or raised floors. The theater portion still has, as it were, along the facing of the back wall the ramp edging of steps leading up to the balcony. The decorations are raggedy and the chandeliers and the sidelight brackets have disappeared. The structural supports in the area of the stage and wings are laid bare, an orchestration of sturdy redwood ribs.

Frank Simas related that plans were afoot to renovate the vacant and dilapidated offices, unused at the moment because of the expense involved to meet fire regulations. In addition, the shades of green on the stuccoed surface at the ground level were being extended to the upper heights, emulating the "cream and spinach" colorations of the Carson Mansion. To add a postscript, a more recent visit to Eureka disclosed that the exterior painting had been completed. And Allan A. McVicar, one of the new owners of the building and a member of the Ingomar Club, informed me that the refurbished professional offices on the upper floors are once again tenanted, reminding one that sometimes history does repeat itself. While the structure has been renamed Carson Block and testifies to the active movement for a journey into the past, thought might well be given to posting a plaque or, as British antiquarians would describe it, a memorial tablet recalling its role as a "temple of the muses." *A National List of Historic Theater Buildings* (1978 edition), compiled by Professor Gene Chesley, member of the Dramatic Art Department at the University of California, Davis, includes an entry on the Ingomar Theatre.

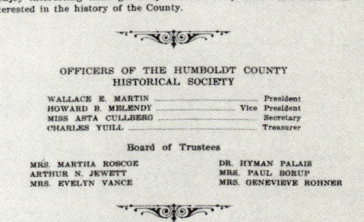

Souvenir Program from final performance in Ingomar Theatre sponsored by the Humboldt County Historical Society.

FILLED WITH OLD MEMORIES—For a good many years I have been compiling information of historic interest concerning our Northwestern California . . . in doing so I have, of course, visited many of the sites concerned in the work. . . .

One place, so close, yet seemingly so far away . . . was the old Imogar theater in the Buhne building. . . .

I mentioned the fact to "Scoop" Beal that I had never seen the old theater . . . then and there, "Scoop" became my guide . . . we traveled the couple of blocks to the old showhouse . . . went through the streamlined hardware department of the Buhne firm . . . through the warehouse . . . up a flight of stairs . . . and we were there. . .

The old architecture of the Imogar is for the most part still there . . . and in its rather unglorious use as a warehouse . . . there is a lot of beauty to be seen.

The fancy plasterwork, which spelled the last word in an amusement place of those days, is still to be seen . . . gold leaf, flowery scrollwork. . . . The arching proscenium with its rows of colored electric bulbs . . . the old-fashioned bulbs are still there. . . . The main floor, the curving balcony and the elegant boxes were designed to seat around 400 people. . . . The velvet trim on the boxes is still there . . . one box, we noticed still had chairs. . . .

The huge stage . . . and it is a big stage . . . could handle almost any size drama, vaudeville, or opera of that period. . . . On the woodwork back of the stage are the scrawled names of old performers who made their appearance here.

The vaudeville and dramatic companies arrived in complete groups on the steamers from San Francisco . . . they could play for a week or more . . . altering their program at least a couple of times. . . . The roomy orchestra pit indicates that there were often musical accompaniments of size.

"Scoop" told me that the old theater was never touched by motion pictures . . . but remained pure in its dramatic and vaudeville heart.

1000 Persons On Sunday At 'Ingomar'
HT 4-15-58

More than 1000 visitors attended the final showing of the old Ingomar Theatre Sunday afternoon, making a total of 3000 people who had visited the theatre during the week.

When the "curtain" fell at 5 o'clock, there were many misty eyes, as nostalgic music rang through the structure. There were three blinks of the old carbon-filamented electric lights, some over 50 years old, announcing the end of the show house. On the stage the Sweet Adelines, directed by Mrs. Helen Throckmorton, sang the farewell.

Besides the Sweet Adelines, the afternoon visitors were entertained by the Eastwood Trio composed of Barbara Harding, Carolyn Doyle, and Mary June Martin. Mrs. Stanley Roscoe gave a 15 minute talk, while the farewell was recorded by Eddie Arnold, who also served as master-of-ceremonies.

A highlight of the closing day was the showing of a large number of Old-time slides

3000 Visited Ingomar Theater
HS 4-15-58

A total of 3,000 persons visited the old Ingomar Theatre during its final curtain call open house last week. More than 1,000 persons visited the landmark Sunday, the final day of its opening.

Slides were shown by Dr. and Mrs. Eugene Fountain of Blue Lake. The Sweet Adelines and the Eastwood Trio provided the music. Mrs. Stanney Roscoe gave a history of the theater and Edward Arnold was master of ceremonies.

Three blinks on the old carbon-filamented electric lights announced the end of the show house. The Humboldt County Historical Society sponsored the open house.

The theater, located at Third and F streets, will be made into a modern furniture mart by Guy Libert, owner of Home Furniture Company.

Curtain Rises Last Time At Old Ingomar

Eureka's famous old Ingomar Theatre opened yesterday afternoon at one o'clock for its last fling, drawing over 150 visitors on its initial "showing."

Newspaper accounts of Final Curtain Call.

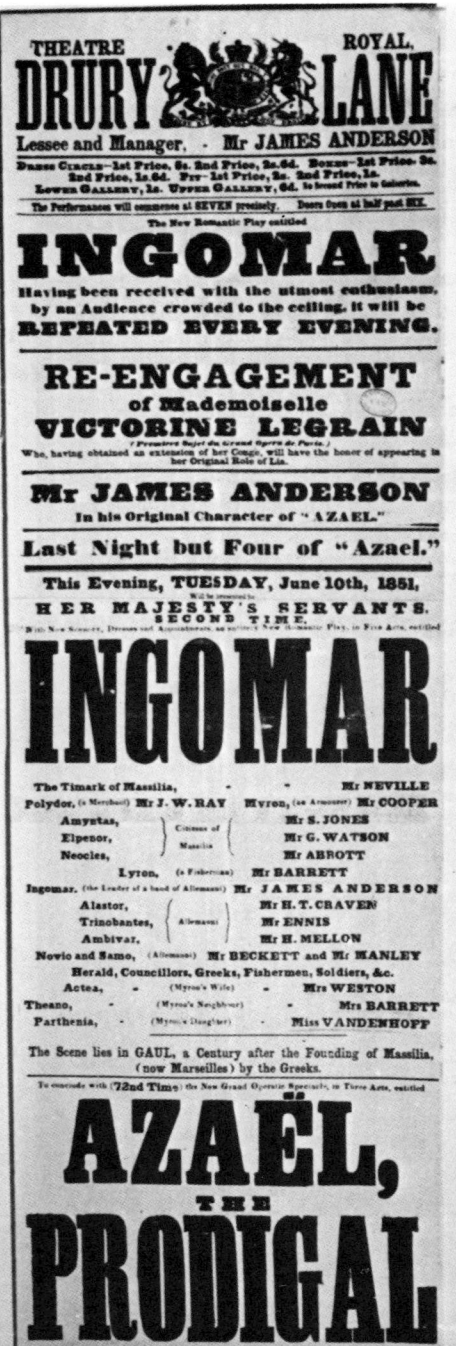
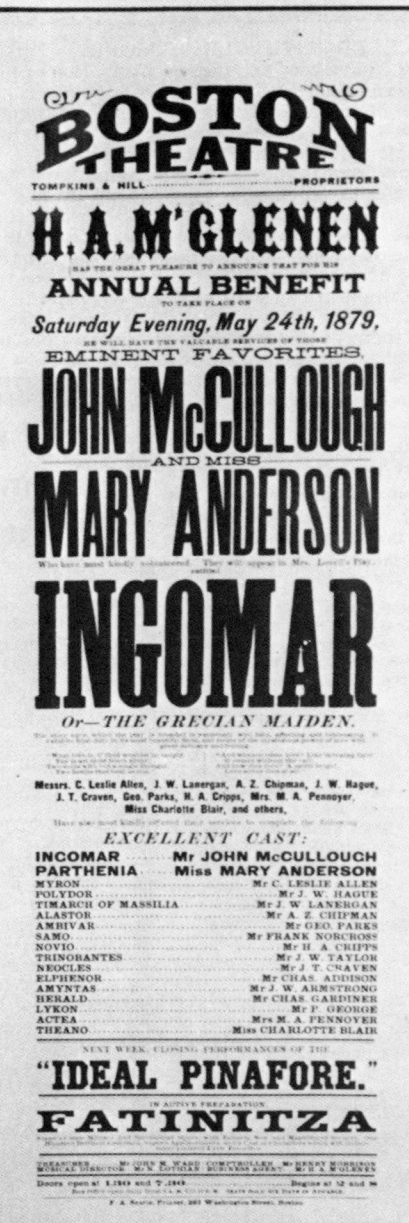

Programs of performances in London and Boston of *Ingomar*.

CHAPTER EIGHT

A TRUSTEE

A Social Precedent

ALTHOUGH THIS CHAPTER is concerned primarily with the Ingomar Club, historical continuity would seem to be best served by a preliminary account of the Humboldt Club. It must be stressed, of course, that there is no direct relationship between the two social groups. The creation of the former occurred a decade after the demise of the latter, albeit the interim lack of such a facility for local business and professional men and their guests must have been felt. Whether some of the members of the Humboldt Club joined the Ingomar Club may be possible but not necessarily an integral part of a new plan. What makes an account of the Humboldt Club desirable is that it provided a precedent, had somewhat the same format, and included the presence of William Carson as a life member and his son John Milton as an active participant. Indeed, upon the death of William Carson, the *Standard* (April 12, 1912) published the very effusive memorial resolution of the Humboldt Club attesting to their pride in his membership.

The existence of such social clubs had been a familiar feature in American cities and Eureka was no exception. The obituary accounts of Carson's death in February 1912 recorded that he had been a life member of the Humboldt Club (although one reporter referred to it as the Eureka Club). It was organized in January 1900, the charter members disbanding the Humboldt Wheelmen, a bicyclists' association. The genesis for broadening the base of membership and social activities was the opportunity to obtain adequate quarters in the proposed Russ building on Third Street. A leading spirit in its formation was Charles Parsons (C. P.) Soule, previously mentioned as a close associate of Carson. In its issue of January 2, 1901, the *Times* carried the report of the club's president, Samuel I. Allard (whose business activities included real estate, abstracts, insurance, and loans), detailing many of the initial facts. Compared to a total of 62 members at the outset—30 resident, 22 non-resident, and 10 life members at $100 each—the total number after one year's existence came to 177—136 residents, 31 non-residents, and still 10 life members. He noted that their quarters were being finished and the fixtures and furniture had been purchased. Particularly of benefit to the community, stressed Allard, was the hospitality and entertainment provided for many visitors in walks of life important to the progress of Eureka.

The *Humboldt County Souvenir* (1904, 2nd ed., pp. 137, 142) includes pictures of the outside of the building as well as of the reading and billiard rooms which to the naked eye suggest spaciousness and luxury. The Steenfott Collection of Photographs at Humboldt State University has an excellent picture of the billiard room and two score members intent upon the games in progress at the two pool tables. The site is listed as the upper floor of the Russ building on Third Street between F and G, the lower floor being occupied by a realty firm and an abstract company. A frequent member elected to the board of directors was John Milton Carson. Meals were served and especially sumptuous were the buffets held every January on the occasion of the club's anniversary. An interesting account in the society column of the short-lived *Daily Eurekan Herald* (February 12, 1910) states that wives were allowed to enter the sacred portals once a year. At this particular party there were 400 guests present and members of the second generation Carson family were in the receiving line. Mrs. Milton Carson was listed as in charge of the room set aside for playing bridge. Her daughters Bell and Marian assisted in the entertainment.

That the times and purposes changed after World War I was reflected in the new activities of the Humboldt Club. Throughout 1919, for example, the *Times* devoted generous space and publicity to its orientation as more of a service club. Its approach was to sponsor weekly luncheons for the promotion of civic projects. Among the topics supported were the construction of a public swimming pool and auditorium, the improvement of street paving and nearby highway roads, the encouragement of a tourist hotel, the creation of a county choral society, and the holding of a musical festival in August. Additional information may be gleaned from the columns of the *Times* in 1923. The issue of January 3 contains an announcement of the election of officers at the New Year's turkey dinner at the quarters on Third Street. More significant was the city-wide drive for new members in February. The objective was to obtain 150 additional members so that the Humboldt Club could "carry out projects." An accompanying statement spelled out the projects as the provision of public recreational facilities, reorganization of the chamber of commerce, and continuance of their weekly luncheons as a forum for the interaction of ideas among business men. But the abbreviated two-day membership campaign, terminated abruptly in favor of a community effort to assure minor league baseball for the coming summer, signed a total of only 54 persons. Obviously new members were not flocking to the call. One inference would seem to be that the international service clubs which had sprung up—Lions, Kiwanis, Rotary, etc.—offered more to civic-minded individuals in the way of worthy human causes.

That the situation had reached a crisis might be deduced from an article in the *Times* (March 6, 1936). The thrust was upon an open house to celebrate an extensive program of improvements to the club's quarters at Third and G Streets. It was announced that the interior had been completely refinished "to renew its activity in the business and social life of Eureka." The hope was expressed that the membership might be increased. The plan called for social gatherings to be held each Thursday evening. And for a while the local newspapers carried the events such as bridge parties and guest speakers. But the decline in the fortunes of the Humboldt Club, it would seem, were not stemmed by these efforts. Meager space was given to its activities in the press. Whatever might have been the ambition to engage in civic service, the role became that of a purely social club. Instead of every anniversary being signalized by a sumptuous banquet, the news items simply read that refreshments were served.

Information gathered from old-timers and knowledgeable persons would indicate that the younger men did not join. The quarters in the Russ building became the refuge of an elderly generation whose daily perspective must have been a steadily-thinning membership as its ranks were riddled by the grim reaper. As Ralph L. Dyer, a local resident, described it, members became aware "of the endless flight of stairs...up which they had to clamber." That the end had come might be deduced from the disappearance of its name and telephone number from the Eureka city directory in 1943 and thereafter. Apparently without any formal public statement the Humboldt Club had disbanded and departed from the scene.

Ingomar Club

How the Ingomar Club came into existence and acquired the Carson Mansion may be traced to the decision of a third-generation member, a granddaughter of William Carson, to put the house on the market for sale.

A TRUSTEE

After the death of the lumber magnate in 1912 the residence had been occupied by the eldest son John Milton and his family. He died in 1941 and his wife in 1944. Their daughter Bell Carson and her husband Clarence La Boyteaux took possession and lived there for several years with their son Ellsworth. Curiously, Baird in his data book report did not make clear the relationship between Mrs. Clarence La Boyteaux and the Carson family. His statement is that "Mr. and Mrs. Clarence La Boyteaux purchased the property in 1944" whereas they inherited it. Whatever the reasons, they decided to move to the San Francisco Bay area. Despite the fame and glamor of the Carson Mansion, no individual family could be found who wanted either to spend the money for its upkeep or to administer such a large house given modern-day servant problems.

A campaign gathered momentum in 1947 among historically-minded citizens, participated in by a newly-formed Humboldt County Historical Society, to have the community purchase it as a showplace for the city of Eureka. The price was understood to be very moderate, the only proviso being that the city pledge a permanency for the heritage of yesteryear. What would seem to have been the stumbling block was the issue of whether the city might not eventually turn the Carson Mansion into a museum for the display of relics. Will N. Speegle, veteran newspaperman, was strongly in favor of the proposal and urged support in his column in the *Times* (July 6, 1947). Incidentally, in 1960 such a museum did become a reality with the establishment of the Clarke Museum at Third and E Streets, in the old Bank of Eureka. At any rate, an editorial in the *Standard* (July 18, 1947) hoped that it would not be torn down or diverted to utilitarian purposes not in keeping with its original character. It ranked along with "the bay, floral beauties, and the redwood . . . as things to see here." Chet Schwarzkopf, a writer for the *Times* (August 17, 1947), responded to the rumor of converting it into a swank night club with the terse utterance, "perish the thought." And disturbing rumors frequently circulated that a freeway might be routed through its location or that it might be remodeled into an apartment building. But the desirable acquisition of the Carson Mansion as a community enterprise did not materialize.

In the meanwhile a new development was in progress. The source is Beal, writing in the *Times-Standard* (December 20, 1970), on the occasion of the twentieth anniversary of the Ingomar Club. J. H. Crothers, publisher of the above newspaper and a member of the Bohemian Club in San Francisco, had lunched with Carl Gustafson, a local automobile dealer. Their conversation (chronicled as sometime in 1949) centered on the need in Eureka for a similar type of place where business and professional men could meet and dine and bring guests. For several months a search was pursued for a suitable site. The La Boyteaux family was contacted as to the possible purchase of the Carson Mansion and the reception was favorable. So the wheels were set in motion and a verbal option was obtained in October 1949. The incredibly low price of $35,000, including some of the Carson furnishings, was agreed upon. Apart from really being a priceless treasure, one commentator believed it would require $2,000,000 to build such a home at current costs. The signatures of seventy charter members were obtained, each agreeing to put up $1,000, part of the aggregate sum to go for the purchase and the rest set aside in the club's treasury for remodeling purposes.

The transfer of the property was consummated on April 1, 1950, both local daily newspapers providing a feature story on the front page. The *Standard* (March 13, 1950) published the commendatory statement issued by Mrs. La Boyteaux:

> "I am immensely pleased and only happy to know that the house—our house—is passing into such fine and capable hands. I think the organization of the club with the house as its home will be given the same care and attention that has been the concern of my family for so many years. The entire idea is a most happy one and I am sure the club will be a credit to Eureka."

Apparently Clarence La Boyteaux became a member of the Ingomar Club, for the official chart posted in the lounge next to the new dining room carries his name with an asterisk denoting "deceased." His son Ellsworth is listed as a non-resident member in the 1976 directory of the social organization (defined as living more than forty miles distant from Eureka).

It might be noted that the family also sold the timber holdings and mills of the Dolbeer and Carson company, finalizing the negotiations on December 16, 1950. And to complete the story of Carson residences in Eureka, the home of the second son of William Carson, Charles Sumner and his wife, at 615 J Street, was sold in 1967. The purchaser was the *Daily Humboldt Times-Standard*, reportedly for the sum of $200,000, and on the site now stands their plant and offices. This home had been built in 1914, also in Gothic style, and possessed lovely landscaping and an interior of rooms lavishly decorated with a wealth of art objects, marbles, velvet drapes, and oriental rugs.

The story is carried further as to origins by a non-resident member of the Ingomar Club, A. J. (Gus) Russell, a partner in a firm which formerly owned and operated the Geneva Lumber Company at Orick. The account is contained in the *Times* (October 24, 1955). He recalled that members assembled on April 13, 1950 for the very first time in the Carson Mansion to select a name. Mrs. La Boyteaux had requested that the Carson surname not be used. Such titles were suggested as Victorian Club, Castle Club, and Harbor Club. Russell argued "that every social club should have a name with a tradition such as [possessed by] the Boston Club of New Orleans, the Friars, the Lambs, and the Lotus of New York, and the Savages of London." His own thought was to capitalize on the Ingomar nomenclature. To that end, through a friend in Boston, a contact was made with a graduate of Radcliffe College who ran down the facts about the play, *Ingomar*.

The summary of the play which Russell passed on to fellow members may be said to be reasonably elucidating and parallels (although with less detail) that related in the chapter on *Ingomar the Barbarian: A Catalyst*. More than that, Russell went to the trouble of amassing a considerable amount of memorabilia for display at the club premises. He had acquired photostatic copies of the playbill for the Drury Theatre performances of 1851 and photographs of the leading actors and actresses in the cast. He had purchased four books recommended as containing references to *Ingomar*: (1) Daniel Frohman, *Memories of a Manager* (published in 1911); (2) Gagey, *History of the San Francisco Stage* (published in 1950); and (3) biographies of Charles Frohman (probably that co-authored by Isaac Frederick Marcosson and Daniel Frohman, his brother, in 1916), and of John Edward McCullough (perhaps that by Susie C. Clark in 1905). Indeed, Russell proceeded to buy every copy of the play he could locate, the final count being fifty-two, all of which he turned over to the Ingomar Club as its property. The Humboldt Room where the special collections are now housed in the new library of the local university was the recipient of a copy. That his diligence was quite thorough can be attested to by the difficulty I encountered initially in running down a copy through the bookstore approach.

Such is the origin of how the Ingomar Club came to adopt its name, hoping to capture a tradition which perpetuated the memory of the Carson era in the ready symbol of his "favorite stage play" and hopefully the sturdy qualities for which it stood. The bylaws were drawn up by the board of directors on May 18, 1950, restricting membership initially to 120 plus a number of non-residents. It would be a non-profit society dedicated especially to the preservation of the Carson Mansion as a heritage of the past. The full complement of objectives embraced good fellowship, social enjoyment, promotion of athletics and related sports of swimming and yachting, and a mutual interest in the fine arts and music. In his speech as reported in the *Standard* (October 24, 1955) Russell expressed the hope that the Ingomar Club would never become just another luncheon club. A worthy project would be cooperation with the Humboldt State College dramatic department in the discovery of talent and the sponsorship of a theatrical group. It would be fitting to present *Ingomar* on the stage or at least for members of a cast to read selected portions of the play.

If this particular liaison has not been realized, it is but fair to say that the Humboldt County Historical Society has been invited to hold its annual dinners in January (on Sunday afternoon) at the Ingomar Club and the programs have often dealt with the life of William Carson. The accounts invariably say that the available dining accommodations, close to 200 tickets, were sold out. As a further indication of the empathy with the Carson tradition, on one occasion, in the spring of 1965, the society held a meeting at the wedding-gift residence of John Milton across the street where the present owner—Robert Madsen—served as host at the refurbished "pink and white lacy Valentine Victorian home." And for the interested public the Ingomar Club has put together an eight-page booklet of photographs in color of several rooms with accompanying commentaries.

Incidentally, the drama department at Humboldt State College did give four performances of *Ingomar* over the weekend of November 4-7, 1971. But the results would appear to have been quite different from those which Russell had envisaged. To begin with, the faculty director is quoted in the school paper, *Lumberjack* (November 3) as saying "Ingomar is archaic as hell [;] it has no real literary value and virtually no intellectual content." He chose to direct the play for the challenge of making *Ingomar* enjoyable to a modern audience despite feeling that it is "badly written." Still, he would say that "it's a colorful active play featuring three sword fights and a lot of rough and tumble action." It would be up to the actors to carry the story "as if they believe in it." Less respectful was a reviewer in the *Lumberjack* (November 10), labeling *Ingomar* as "lightweight all the way." He noted the care taken to remind the audience of the local historical context. Before the opening curtain a short film in color showed the Carson Mansion "in all its Baroque finery" accompanied by slides of gala productions of *Ingomar* in days gone by. Apart from commending the actors, the sets, and the costumes as all quite authentic, the reviewer likened the play to a "television western." If the title were changed to "Ingomar, Son of the Wildwest," the hero put in a cowboy outfit, the sword replaced with a six-shooter, and the set changed to a wild west town, the concoction would emerge a mere western movie. One can only assume that such a statement as "the heroine's utter goodness oozes out all over the set like a sticky cream puff" is meant to demolish any allegiance to the pseudo-classicism indulged in during the nineteenth century.

Truly one might have wished that both the director and the reviewer had examined in depth the classical framework into which *Ingomar* had been pinned. Whether the word "archaic" is defined in terms of the play's theme or of the stilted dialogue extracted in translation from the original German tongue, a more relevant approach might have been to relate the play to Aristotle's observations of what were the canons for good drama in his time. Obviously the play did not aim at comedy which represented men as worse than they are or tragedy which represented men as better than they are. Rather what makes the play pseudo-classicism is that the author (and the translator) preferred to provide homilies and lessons from the past as a guide to maturity. But to make of *Ingomar* a mere variation of a western movie seems a narrow grasp of the theater's potentialities. To put it another way, even if the play might have had overwritten characters, a grounding in the manners and *mores* of the classical period would have furnished a more dignified challenge in bringing *Ingomar* to the stage. As it was, the burden placed upon the cast to resurrect a presumed outdated story seems to straddle the responsibility of wrestling with a bygone era and mastering its subtleties and nuances. Surely the flexibility of theatrical technique today could find new ways of applying the poetic qualities dominant in the classical drama even to a generation attuned more to the conversational style in vogue on the contemporary stage.

The subsequent annals of the Ingomar Club produce some interesting data. The official roster of membership for 1973 lists 251 residents with addresses in communities all over Humboldt County and 47 non-residents (mostly from other cities in California plus a few from Oregon, Washington, Ohio, and Arizona). The maximum limit has been set at 250 residents and 50 non-residents and it is stated that a waiting list has accumulated. The major alteration to the structure for normal club facilities was the construction, on the bay side, of a dining room annex to handle some 200 diners and which included a bar and a lounge. While the annex is modernistic and has its own entrance, the intervening miniature woods assure a shield and so the overall profile is not disturbed. It might be noted that this addition relieved the strain on the parlor, music room, and family dining room (including the extra round table) which were being used for luncheons and dinners. The modest-sized lounge in particular is an attractive room and provides the entrance into the dining room. Perhaps for antiquarian as well as functional purposes, there are two hatracks with mirrors, a coat hanger, and an umbrella stand, for they can service only a few people. A separate cloakroom is close by. There are two lovely canvasses hung on the walls, one in pen and some coloring and the other a water color, both portraying the Carson Mansion as it looks at night when all the rooms are lit up. The warmth and glow of the room with its paneled woodwork lends a sense of cordiality just as the Carson Mansion must have once impressed the visitor as a very liveable home for a family.

A number of minor changes and additions are worth mentioning. Outside, projecting from the front porch entrance is a canopy in the familiar greenish color and sporting a fashionable monogrammed letter "I". On each end of the lawn there is a signpost driven into the ground stating that the residence is the private property of the Ingomar Club. The exterior is periodically repainted and one account notes that it has been done three times since 1950. In the private garden the principal innovation has been the installation of a swimming pool. Inside, the large oil painting of the schooner *William Carson* has been transferred from the parlor to the wall of the new dining room (but on my last visit had been removed for safekeeping). The nameplate of the Ingomar Theatre now graces a prominent spot on the wall alongside the grand staircase. The serving and kitchen facilities have been enlarged to care for the increased number of diners. Upstairs a second bar has been set up in what was once a bedroom and still another bedroom has been turned into the manager's office. The other bedrooms are now lounges where members may indulge in the relaxation of card games, chess, checkers, dominoes, and conversation. For the rest, there have been renovations and replacements of wall paper with grass cloth or matting and new carpets, furnishings, and light fixtures throughout the interior.

The ballroom on the third floor has been given over to pool tables and what was once the billiard room still has its pool table but appears unused. One servant's quarters has been renovated to display club memorabilia, notably photographs recalling memories of the past—members, parties, events. The servant's bedroom next to the ballroom has been fashioned into an historic room for the exhibition of antiquarian memorabilia. Clothes dating back to the first generation of the Carsons include a child's red dress and costumes attributed to his wife—a full length dress, cape, and coat all in black and elaborately woven. Prominently featured is the brown, tight-fitting wedding gown of Sarah Wilson. On one occasion, dated as eighty-five years later (about 1949), it was modeled in a fashion show on May 12 for a brides' tea sponsored by the St. Elizabeth Guild and held at the local Women's Club. Recent acquisitions adorning the vintage bed are a pillow-case and a bedspread embroidered with lacy effects used by earlier generations. Then there are displayed an umbrella rack of ancient vintage and a ceremonial sword believed to bear the insignia of the Knights of Pythias. All these items and several family portraits and books were donated a few years ago by Ellsworth La Boyteaux.

Most unique are the so-called Ingomar Plaques which chronologically relate the story of civilization in America in terms of the forest as the progenitor. Dr. Samuel P. Burre, a local physician, was not only the author of the booklet versifying the ages of mankind but also the artist responsible for carving the relief plaques from the woods of the neighboring timberland. The last of the twelve plaques is called "America in Bloom," showing the Carson Mansion in silhouette with planes above and cars and people below. He gave the twelve plaques as a gift to the Ingomar Club and they adorn the walls in the ballroom. They are a poignant reminder of the role which Carson played in the utilization of the redwood for human survival above the level of primitive surroundings.

For the public, of course, the major concern is the exterior and the Ingomar Club would seem to be very mindful of its responsibility to preserve the Carson Mansion as a scenario of delight to tens of thousands. It has been mentioned before that the Historic American Buildings Survey assembled for its records a data book report of seven pages and twenty-eight photographs of the Carson Mansion in 1964. But thus far the United States National Park Service has not included it in the National Register of Historic Places. This accreditation is based upon the National Historic Preservation Act of 1966 by which the owner of such a property is offered a certificate and a bronze plaque designating it a National Historic Landmark. In return the owner agrees to preserve those significant historic values for which it is singled out. Publication of the accumulative list is compiled in book form periodically and as of now there have been printed editions in 1969, 1972, 1974, and 1976. Presumably, if the Ingomar Club would wish to initiate such a request, it could certainly meet the requirements. Lately the department of the interior announced that President Carter's National Heritage Program will be transferred from the National Park Service to the newly-created Heritage Conservation and Recreation Service.

Recently a major issue has been the question of sex discrimination. The rules of the Ingomar Club restrict the presence of women guests to Sundays and special occasions. The suit filed by the state office of the attorney-general is based on the traumatic experience of the female vice-chairperson of the California Coastal Zone Conservation Commission. The board was in Eureka on official state business in October 1973 and an informal tour of Carson Mansion was organized for them. But the woman member was refused admission and in what she described as humiliating circumstances had to remain outside. She charged that it was "an infringement of my civil rights and an impairment to fulfilling my duties as an officer of the State of California." The attorney-general's office called the episode a violation of the Unruh Civil Rights Act of 1961 which prohibits discrimination in places of public accommodation. The fact that members of the Ingomar Club were permitted to bring guests during the weekdays, even if only males, established the premises as semi-public. Furthermore, the concept of not allowing women, especially professional women, to enter the club, deprived them of participation in a community's business and political life. The Ingomar Club refused to retreat and voted to defend its guest policy even though knowing that court action would be instituted. However, on February 28, 1978, an out-of-court settlement was concluded, permitting female guests the right to enter for any business, civic, or political function. But the ban on female membership remained intact since the state law did not prevent a private social club from barring applicants on the grounds of sex, religion, or race.

To conclude, what can be said for the accomplishments of the generation passing through a colonial stage of cultural existence? Obviously one is dealing with intangibles and at best the responses must be speculative. That Carson and fellow travellers did their part to raise the sights of their community beyond the daily grapple with obstinate nature cannot be gainsaid. Certainly for those conscious of nobler visions in life the opportunities to indulge had been made available. What one must be painfully aware of is that a sense of cultural refinement drips down to layers of society at a snail's pace. Indeed, it is an everlasting struggle even today to involve sophisticated communities in levels of artistic developments that challenge the mind and nurture the attributes of humanism. A chance reading of a biography of Thackeray by Gordon N. Ray (1955, I, p. 216) offered an opportunity of recourse to the classical period itself for an assay of the aesthetic approach. The English novelist is cited as providing a colorful translation of the Roman poet Ovid (*Epistulae Ex Ponto*, Book II, No. IX, line 47) to the effect of a tribute to the "ingenuous arts which prevent the ferocity of the manners and act as an emollient." A more conventional rendition of the Latin words in English is to be found in the *Oxford Dictionary of Quotations* (1953, 2nd ed., p. 372): "Note too that a faithful study of the liberal arts humanizes character and permits it not to be cruel." At any rate, it could not be said of Humboldt County and its metropolis of Eureka that in the second half of the nineteenth century there had been an indifference to the cultivation of man as a creature capable of earthly dignity.

In the meanwhile students of acculturation may well ponder such strange bedfellows as the drama in pseudo-classical garb and architecture in adulterated Gothic Revival habit clasping hands to penetrate the armor of frontier life on behalf of civilization as the norm might be conceived in the nineteenth century.

Eureka, California (1905).

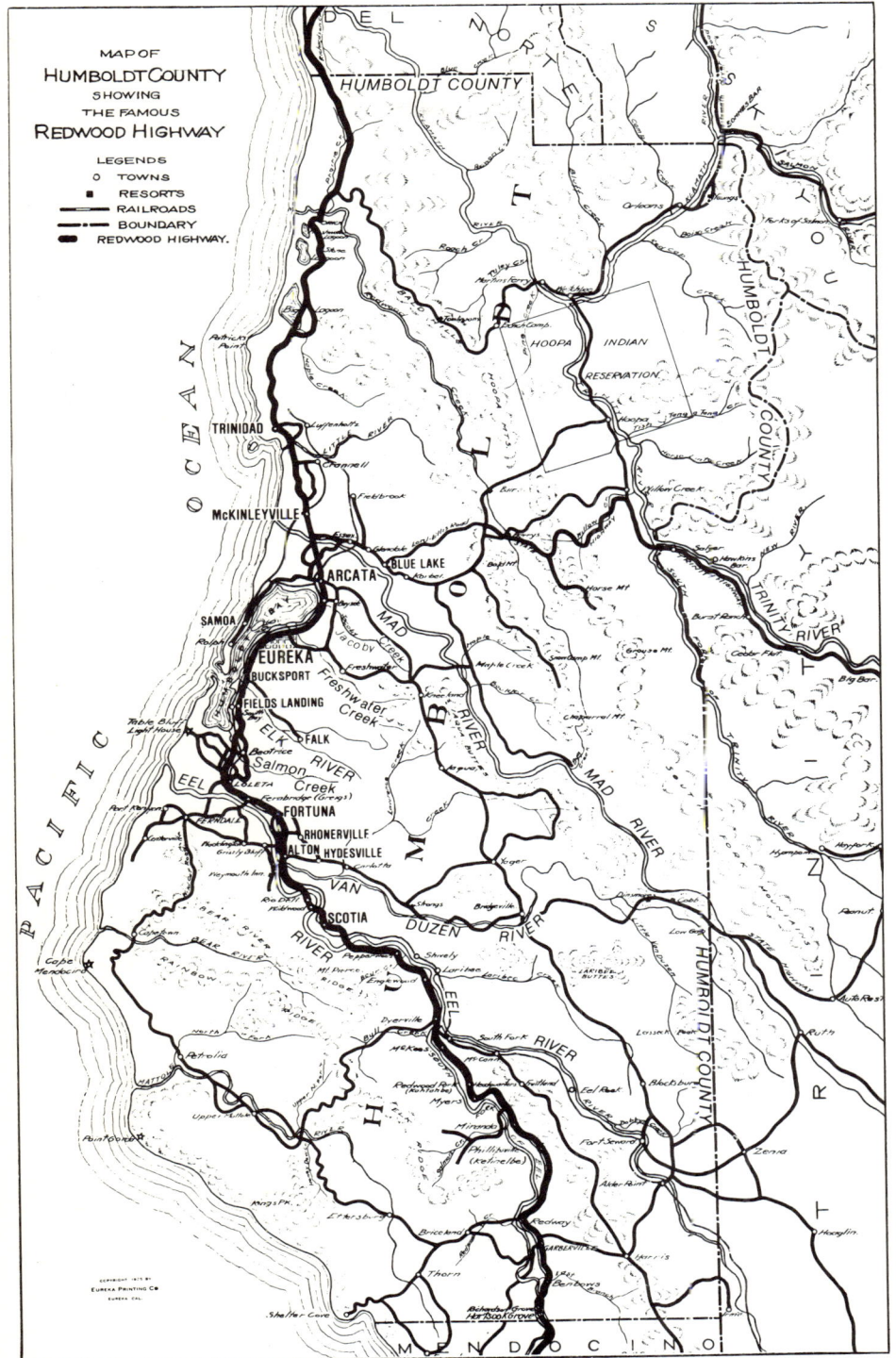

Bibliography

PRIMARY SOURCES

SPECIAL COLLECTIONS ROOM - HUMBOLDT STATE UNIVERSITY

Chamber of Commerce, Eureka, 1883, etc.
Humboldt County Collection.
Humboldt County Historical Society, Journal, 1948, 1954.
Humboldt Historian, 1953 to present. Originally known as the *Humboldt Newsletter.* Both are publications of the Humboldt County Historical Society.
Steenfott Collection of Photographs.
Susie Baker Fountain Papers, 119 volumes, mostly newspaper clippings and often neither dated nor identified. The useful volumes for this study were 2, 28, 30, 31, 59, and 64.

BANCROFT LIBRARY

Dolbeer and Carson Lumber Company, Business Papers (circa 1884-1951), 56 volumes. Includes records of the Bucksport and Elk River Railroad Company, the Humboldt Northern Railway Company, and the William Carson Estate Company. For this study the most useful volumes were those which possess the cash receipts and collections, both of the lumber company and personal items. vol. I (1887-1890), vol. II (1891-1900), vol. III (1900-1907), and vol. IV (1907-1915).

NEWSPAPERS.

The files held by Humboldt State University and the California State Library at Sacramento were the fullest. The Bancroft Library at Berkeley has some reels plus a number of broken files of short-lived newspapers. Only the major newspapers are listed:
Weekly Humboldt Times, 1854-1908.
Daily Humboldt Times, 1874-1883.
Daily Humboldt Times-Telephone, 1883-1886.

BIBLIOGRAPHY

Daily Humboldt Times, 1867-1967.
Weekly Humboldt Standard, 1888-1898.
Semi-Weekly Humboldt Standard, 1899-1905.
Daily Humboldt Standard, 1884-1967.
Daily Humboldt Times-Standard, 1968-present.

CALIFORNIA ARCHITECT AND BUILDING NEWS (San Francisco), 1882-1900.

Preceded by the *Quarterly Architectural Review* (1879) and the *California Architect and Building Review* (1880-1881). Both the San Diego Historical Society Archives and the Bancroft Library possess this monthly journal.

ARTICLES

Andrews, Wayne. "The Impatient Evolution of the American House." *House Beautiful*. Feb. 1965, pp. 90-105.
Bangert, Ethel E. "A Backward Glance at Eureka." *California Highway Patrolman*. March 1950, pp. 22, 71-73.
Beringer, Pierre N. "Humboldt County." *Overland Monthly*, Jan. 1909, pp. 74-82.
Beronius, George. "Humboldt County: California's Last Frontier." *Los Angeles Times* (home section), Sunday, Jan. 18, 1976, cover page and pp. 6, 8-13.
Gerster, Georg. "Das Carson-Haus in Eureka." *Bawelt* (Berlin), April 21, 1969, pp. 517-519.
Gordon, David E. "Humboldt Lumber Mills." *Wood and Iron*, August 1904, No. 2, pp. 10-11.
Hildebrand, J. R. "California's Coastal Redwood Realm." *National Geographic Magazine*, Feb. 1939, pp. 133-184.
Historic American Buildings Survey, "Photograph—Data Book Report," 1964, 7 pp. Prepared by Joseph A. Baird, Jr.
Johnston, Richard. "The Carson Home: An Example of Victorian Charm." *San Francisco Chronicle* (Bonanza section), Sunday, July 31, 1960, pp. 6-7.
Melendy, H. Brett. "Two Men and a Mill: John Dolbeer, William Carson, and the Redwood Lumber Industry in California." California *Historical Society Quarterly (1959), No. 1, pp. 59-71.*
Palais, Hyman and Earl Roberts. "The History of the Lumber Industry in Humboldt County." *Pacific Historical Review*, XIX, No. 1, Feb. 1950, pp. 1-16.
Perusse, Lyle F. "The Gothic Revival in California, 1850-1890." *Journal of the Society of Architectural Historians*, XIV, No. 3, Oct. 1955, pp. 15-22.
"Samuel Newsom: An Obituary." *Architect and Engineer*, XIV, Sept. 1908, p. 79.
"The Carson Mansion, Eureka, California." *Michigan Society of Architects, Monthly Bulletin*, May 1959, pp. 12-13.
"The Old Houses are Reminders of Eureka's Lumbering Past." *Sunset Magazine* (central section edition), Oct. 1970, pp. 59-61.
White, Douglas and William A. Lawson. "Northern California." *Harper's Weekly*, Dec. 26, 1903, pp. 2099-2114.
"William Carson: An Obituary." *Pioneer Western Lumberman*, vol. 57, No. 2, March 1, 1912, p. 7.

BIBLIOGRAPHY

BOOKS

Bancroft, Hubert Howe. *The Works of Hubert Howe Bancroft: History of California, 1848-1890*. Reprint. Vols. VI and VII. Santa Barbara: 1970.

Beal, Lawrence "Scoop". *Carson's Redwood Castle: The Carson Mansion, America's Finest Victorian Home and the Man Who Built It*. Eureka: 1973. 23 pp.

Bettendorf, Frank Bernard. "Dramatic Activities of the Humboldt Bay Area, 1880 to 1912." Unpublished thesis, U.C.L.A., 1963. 141 pp.

Burre, Samuel P., M.D. *The Plaques of Ingomar*. Eureka: 1956. 38 pp.

Carr, John. *Pioneer Days in California*. Eureka: 1891. 452 pp.

Cherry, Edgar and Company. *Redwood and Lumbering in California Forests, With Illustrations*. San Francisco: 1884. 107 pp.

Cox, Thomas R. *Mills and Markets: A History of the Pacific Coast Lumber Industry to 1900*. Seattle: 1974. 332 pp.

Coy, Owen C. *The Humboldt Bay Region, 1850-1875*. Los Angeles: 1929. 346 pp.

Eddy, J. M., compiler. *In the Redwood's Realm*. San Francisco: 1893. 112 pp. Prepared for the Chamber of Commerce.

Federal Writers' Project. *California: A Guide to the Golden State*. Rev. eds. New York: 1954, 1967.

Genzoli, Andrew M. "Christ Church: The Reward of a Pioneer's Faith, A Centennial History, 1870-1970." 1970. Unpublished. 122 pp.

———. *Redwood Country: Legacy of the Pioneer*. Eureka: 1973. 79 pp.

Genzoli, Andrew M. and Wallace E. Martin. *Redwood Bonanza: A Frontier's Reward*. Eureka: 1967. 76 pp.

———. *Redwood Frontier: Wilderness Defiant*. Eureka: 1961. 56 pp.

Gibbs, Jim. *West Coast Windjammers In Story and Pictures*. Seattle: 1968. 192 pp.

Hamm, Lillie E. *History and Business Directory of Humboldt County*. Eureka: 1890. 226 pp.

History of Humboldt County, California, With Illustrations. San Francisco: Wallace W. Elliott and Co., 1882. 220 pp.

Humboldt County Souvenir. Eureka: Board of Supervisors, 1902. 192 pp.

Humboldt County Souvenir. 2nd ed. Eureka: Board of Supervisors, 1904. 210 pp.

Humboldt Times Centennial Edition. A Century of Progress, 1854-1954. February 1954. 387 pp.

Ingomar Club. Eureka: circa 1970. 8 pp.

Ingomar Club Directory. Eureka: 1976. 50 pp.

Irvine, Leigh Hadley. *History of Humboldt County, California, With Biographical Sketches*. Los Angeles: 1915. 1290 pp.

Kneiss, Gilbert H. *Redwood Railways: A Story of Redwoods, Picnics, and Commuters*. Berkeley: 1956. 165 pp.

Kyne, Peter B. *The Valley of the Giants*. New York: 1919. 388 pp.

Lovell, Maria, trans. *Ingomar the Barbarian: A Play in Five Acts*. Boston: 1896. 64 pp. William Warren Edition of Standard Plays.

Melendy, Howard Brett. "One Hundred Years of the Redwood Lumber Industry, 1850-1950." Unpublished doctoral dissertation, Stanford University, 1952. 377 pp.

McGowan, Thomas. "Christ Church History, 1869-1964." 1964. Unpublished. 58 pp.

Newsom, Joseph Cather. *Artistic Buildings and Homes of Los Angeles.* 20 plates. Los Angeles: circa 1889.

Newsom, Joseph Cather. *Modern Homes of California.* No. 4, about 100 plates and sketches. San Francisco: circa 1893.

———. *Picturesque and Artistic Homes and Buildings of California.* No. 3, about 100 plates. San Francisco: circa 1890.

Newsom, Samuel. *Some City and Suburban Homes.* 50 plates. San Francisco: circa 1890.

Newsom, Samuel and Joseph Cather. *Picturesque California Homes.* No. 1, 35 plates. San Francisco: circa 1884. A reprint of this volume was published in 1978 by Hennessey and Ingalls, Inc., Los Angeles, with an introduction by David Gebhard.

———. *Picturesque California Homes.* No. 2, 40 plates. San Francisco: circa 1887.

Palmquist, Peter E. *Fine California Views: The Photographs of A. W. Ericson.* Eureka: 1975. 111 pp.

Parker, J. Carlyle. *An Annotated Bibliography of the History of Del Norte and Humboldt Counties.* Humboldt State College Library: 1960. 89 pp. Begun by R. Dean Galloway.

Ship Registries and Enrollments: Port of Eureka, California, 1859-1920. San Francisco: 1941. 167 pp. (Dates given on cover are 1864-1940, with which entries correspond more closely than with those dates given on the title page.) Compiled by Survey of Federal Archives, Work Projects Administration.

Thornbury, Delmar L. *California's Redwood Wonderland, Humboldt County.* San Francisco: 1923. 167 pp.

Wattenburger, Ralph Thomas. "The Redwood Lumbering Industry on the Northern California Coast, 1850-1900." Unpublished master's thesis, University of California, Berkeley, 1931. 87 pp.

REFERENCE MATERIALS

ARCHITECTURE

Aidala, Thomas. *The Great Houses of San Francisco.* New York: 1974.

Andrews, Ralph W. *Glory Days of Logging.* Seattle: 1956.

———. *Photographers of the Frontier West: Their Lives and Works, 1875 to 1915.* Seattle: 1965.

———. *Picture Gallery Pioneers, 1850 to 1875.* Seattle: 1964.

———. *Redwood Classic.* New York: 1958.

Andrews, Wayne. *Architecture in America: A Photographic History from the Colonial Period to the Present.* New York: 1960.

Baird, Joseph Armstrong, Jr. *Time's Wondrous Changes: San Francisco Architecture, 1766-1915.* San Francisco: California Historical Society, 1960.

Bangs, Edward Geoffrey. *Portals West: A Folio of Late Nineteenth Century Architecture in California.* San Francisco: California Historical Society, 1960.

Comstock, Helen. *America's Furniture: Seventeenth, Eighteenth, Nineteenth Century Styles.* New York: 1962.

BIBLIOGRAPHY

Da Costa, Beverley, ed. *Historic Houses of America Open to the Public.* New York: 1969.

Davidson, Marshall, ed. *The American Heritage History of Antiques from the Civil War to World War I.* New York: 1969.

———. *The American Heritage History of Notable American Houses.* New York: 1971.

Folsom, Merrill. *More Great American Mansions and Their Stories.* New York: 1967.

Gebhard, David, Roger Montgomery, Robert Winter, John and Sally Woodbridge. *A Guide to Architecture in San Francisco and Northern California.* Santa Barbara: 1973.

Gebhard, David and Harriette von Breton. *Architecture in California, 1868-1968: An Exhibition.* Salt Lake City: 1968.

Gebhard, David and Robert Winter. *A Guide to Architecture in Los Angeles and Southern California.* Salt Lake City: 1977.

Karp, Ben. *Wood Motifs in American Domestic Architecture: "Phantasy in Wood."* New York: 1966.

Kirker, Harold. "California Architecture and Its Relation to Contemporary Trends in Europe and America" in George Knoles, ed. *Essays and Assays: California History Reappraised*, pp. 91-108. San Francisco: 1973.

———. "California Architecture in the Nineteenth Century: A Social History." Unpublished doctoral dissertation, University of California, Berkeley, 1957.

———. *California's Architectural Frontier: Style and Tradition in the Nineteenth Century.* San Marino: 1960.

Lewis, Oscar. *Here Lived the Californians.* New York: 1957.

Lynes, Russell. *The Domesticated Americans.* New York: 1957.

Maass, John. *The Gingerbread Age: A View of Victorian America.* New York: 1957.

———. *The Victorian Home in America.* New York: 1972.

Pickering, Ernest. *The Homes of America As They Have Expressed the Lives of Our People for Three Centuries.* New York: 1951.

Richey, Elinor. *Remain To Be Seen: Historic California Houses Open to the Public.* Berkeley: 1973.

———. *The Ultimate Victorians of the Continental Side of San Francisco Bay.* Berkeley: 1970.

Rogers, Meyric R. *American Interior Design: The Traditions and Development of Domestic Design from Colonial Times to the Present.* New York: 1947.

Schmidt, Carl F. *The Victorian Era in the United States.* Scottsville, New York: 1971.

Smith, George Everard Kidder. *A Pictorial History of Architecture in America.* New York: 1976. 2 vols.

Vail, Wesley D. *Victorians: An Account of Domestic Architecture in Victorian San Francisco, 1870-1890.* San Francisco: 1964.

———. *San Francisco Victorians: An Account of Domestic Architecture in Victorian San Francisco, 1870-1890.* 2d ed., rev. Sebastopol: 1978.

Wrenn, Tony P. and Elizabeth D. Mulloy. *America's Forgotten Architecture.* New York: 1976.

BIBLIOGRAPHY

THEATER

Brown, Thomas Allston. *A History of the New York Stage: From the First Performance in 1732 to 1901.* New York: 1903. Reissue, 3 vols., 1964.

Chesley, Gene, compiler. *The National List of Historic Theatre Buildings.* 1978 edition. 23 pp.

Gaer, Joseph, ed. *The Theatre of the Gold Rush Decade in San Francisco.* California Literary Research: April 8, 1935. Monograph #5, 99 pp., typewritten manuscript listing plays, operas, minstrel shows, etc., from 1850 to 1859.

Gagey, Edmond M. *The San Francisco Stage: A History.* New York: Columbia University, 1950.

Hart, Jerome. *In Our Second Century.* San Francisco: 1931.

Ireland, Joseph Norton. *Records of the New York Stage from 1750 to 1860.* New York: 1866. Reissue, 2 vols., 1966.

McMinn, George Rupert. *The Theater of the Golden Era in California.* Caldwell, Idaho: 1941.

North California Writers' Project. "History of the San Francisco Theatre: Famous Playhouses of San Francisco, 1861-1875." Vol. XVI, part two. Unpublished, n.d.

Odell, George C. *Annals of the New York Stage.* 15 vols. From 1790s to 1894. New York: 1949.

Rourke, Constance. *Troupers of the Gold Coast.* New York: 1928.

Winter, William. *Vagrant Memories: Being Further Recollections of Other Days.* New York: 1915.

———. *The Wallet of Time.* 2 vols. New York: 1913.

Photographic References

EXTERIOR OF CARSON MANSION

Andrews, Ralph W. *Redwood Classic* (1958), p. 140.
Andrews, Wayne. *Architecture in America* (1960), p. 78.
Atkeson, Roy and David Muench. *California* (1970), p. 75.
Bangs, E. Geoffrey. *Portals West* (1960), p. 24, plate 5.
Beal, Lawrence. *Carson's Redwood Castle* (1973), *passim*.
Da Costa, Beverley, ed. *Historic Houses of America Open to the Public* (1971), p. 23.
Davidson, Marshall B., ed. *American Heritage History of Antiques From the Civil War to World War I* (1969), p. 312, plate 425.
Daily Humboldt Standard, March 13, 1950.
Daily Humboldt Times, July 6, Aug. 17, 1947 and March 12, 1950.
Eddy, J. M., compiler. *In the Redwood's Realm* (1893), p. 87.
Folsom, Merrill. *More Great American Mansions* (1967), p. 165.
Historic American Buildings Survey (1964), Nos. 1-14
Humboldt County Souvenir (1904, 2nd ed.), p. 15.
Ingomar Club (circa 1970), p. 1.
Kirker, Harold. *California's Architectural Frontier* (1960), plate 51.
Lewis, Oscar. *Here Lived the Californians* (1957), p. 141.
Lynes, Russell. *The Domestic Americans* (1957), p. 148.
Maass, John. *The Gingerbread Age* (1957), p. 79.
Maass, John. *The Victorian Home in America* (1972), p. 165 and plates XXIII and XXIV.
Nixon, Stuart. *Redwood Empire* (1966), pp. 89, 184.
Palmquist, Peter E. *Fine California Views: The Photographs of A. W. Ericson* (1975), p. 45.
Richey, Elinor. *Remain To Be Seen: Historic Houses Open to the Public* (1973), p. 156.
Smith, G. E. Kidder, *A Pictorial History of Architecture in America* (1976), II, pp. 758-759.
Sunset Pictorial. *Discovering the California Coast* (1975), p. 36.
"The Carson House: Eureka, California," *Michigan Society of Architects, Monthly Bulletin*, May 1959, pp. 12-13, two photos.

Vail, Wesley D. *Victorians: An Account of Domestic Architecture in Victorian San Francisco* (1964), pp. 46-47.
Vail, Wesley D., *San Franciscan Victorians* (2nd ed. rev., 1978), pp. 93-95.
Wrenn, Tony P. and Elizabeth D. Mulloy. *America's Forgotten Architecture* (1976), p. 73.

FRONT ELEVATION SKETCH BY THE NEWSOMS

Davidson, Marshall B., ed. *American Heritage of Notable American Houses* (1971), p. 261.
Gebhard, David and Harriette von Breton. *Architecture in California, 1868-1968* (1968), plate 21.
Historic American Buldings Survey (1964), No. 28.
Kirker, Harold. *California's Architectural Frontier* (1960), plate 50.
Maass, John. *The Victorian Home in America* (1972), p. 164.
Newsom, Samuel and Joseph Cather. *Picturesque California Homes* (circa 1887), No. 2, plate 40.
Vail, Wesley D. *Victorians: An Account of Domestic Architecture in Victorian San Francisco* (1964), p. 29.
Vail, Wesley D., *San Franciscan Victorians* (2nd ed. rev., 1978), p. 92.

INTERIOR OF CARSON MANSION

Andrews, Wayne. *Architecture in America* (1960), p. 78.
Beal, Lawrence. *Carson's Redwood Castle* (1973), *passim*.
Daily Humboldt Standard, March 13, 1950.
Daily Humboldt Times, March 12, 1950.
Folsom, Merrill. *More Great American Mansions* (1967), p. 167.
Historic American Buildings Survey (1964), Nos. 15-27.
Ingomar Club (circa 1970), *passim*.
Maass, John. *The Victorian Home in America* (1972), p. 166.
Nixon, Stuart. *Redwood Empire* (1966), p. 185.
"The Carson Mansion, Eureka, California," *Michigan Society of Architects, Monthly Bulletin*, May 1959, p. 13.
Vail, Wesley D. *Victorians: An Account of Domestic Architecture in Victorian San Francisco* (1964), p. 45.
Vail, Wesley D., *San Franciscan Victorians* (2nd ed. rev., 1978), pp. 132, 135.

PHOTOGRAPHS OF WILLIAM CARSON

Daily Humboldt Standard, Feb. 20, 1912.
Daily Humboldt Times, Feb. 20, 1912.
Gordon, David E. "Humboldt Lumber Mills," *Wood and Iron*, July 1904, No. 1, p. 10.

CARSON BLOCK

Daily Humboldt Standard, Dec. 31, 1891.
Daily Humboldt Times, Dec. 23, 1892.
Eddy, J. M., compiler. *In the Redwood's Realm* (1893), pp. 29, 94.
Humboldt County Souvenir (1904, 2nd ed.), p. 147.
Steenfott Collection of Photographs, Humboldt State University Library.

INTERIOR OF INGOMAR THEATRE

Bettendorf, Frank Bernard. *Dramatic Activities of the Humboldt Bay, 1880 to 1912* (1963), back pages.
Daily Humboldt Standard, April 7, 1958.
Daily Humboldt Times, December 23, 1892 and April 9, 1958.
Humboldt County Souvenir (1904, 2nd ed.), p. 147.

MILTON CARSON'S HOUSE

Lynes, Russell. *The Domesticated Americans* (1957), p. 148.
Maass, John. *The Victorian Home in America* (1972), p. 167 and plate XXV.
Richey, Elinor. *Remain To Be Seen: Historic Houses Open to the Public* (1973), p. 156.
Sunset Pictorial. *Discovering the California Coast* (1975), p. 35.

RUSS BUILDING—QUARTERS OF HUMBOLDT CLUB

Humboldt County Souvenir (1904, 2nd ed.), p. 142.
Steenfott Collection of Photographs, Humboldt State University Library.

MAPS OF HUMBOLDT COUNTY

Hoopes, Chad L. *Lure of Humboldt Bay Region* (1966), p. 1.
Humboldt County Souvenir (1904, 2nd ed.), frontispiece.
Melendy, Howard Brett. *One Hundred Years of the Redwood Industry, 1850-1950* (1952), pp. 150, 166, 174.

Index

CARSON CLAN (in order of generations)

FIRST GENERATION

Carson, William
  entrepreneur, 1, 11-23, 124, 137
  residence, xv, 39, 43-44, 53, 61, 73-79
  theater, 6, 93, 95-96, 99, 105-106, 112-113, 120, 125, 129-131
Carson, Mrs. William (née Sarah Wilson), 20-22, 61, 73, 75, 81, 145

SECOND GENERATION

Carson, John Milton, 2, 4, 21, 23, 24, 42-43, 56-59, 61, 124, 131, 137-138, 140, 143
Carson, Mrs. John Milton (née Mary Bell), 21, 56, 59, 61, 138
Carson, Carlotta (Mrs. Robert James Tyson, Sr.), 16, 21, 24-25, 57, 81
Carson, Charles Sumner, 19, 21, 23, 24, 141
Carson, Mrs. Charles Sumner (née Amelia Ohman), 21
Carson, William Wilson, 21, 23, 24, 25

THIRD GENERATION

Carson, Sarah Bell (Mrs. Clarence La Boyteaux), 24, 26, 58, 138, 139, 140, 141
Carson, Marian (Mrs. Sam Milton Haley), 24, 25-26, 138
Tyson, William Carson, 24-25, 26
Tyson, Mrs. William Carson (née Irene Hogdon), 25, 26
Tyson, Robert James, Jr., 24-25

FOURTH GENERATION

La Boyteaux, Ellsworth, 26, 140, 141, 145

HUMBOLDT COUNTY

TOWNSPEOPLE

Allard, Samuel I., 138
Atkinson, Miss L., 95
Beal, Lawrence (Scoop), 1, 6, 56, 140
Bergen, B., 95
Bettendorf, Frank Bernard, 95, 125, 128, 130, 132

INDEX

Bledsoe, A. J., xvi, 90
Bridges, Lloyd, 43
Buhne, Hans Henry, 74, 75
Burre, Samuel P., 145

Carr, John, 12, 19
Carr, Miss Mary, 19
Chase, Miss Rhoda, 108
Chope, A. H., 95
Cox, J. M., 20
Crichton, J. L., 95
Crothers, J. H., 140
Culberg, Asta, 132
Cutten, David, 90

Dauphiny, Ralph L., 90
Dever, Lawrence, xii
Dolbeer, John, 14-15, 17, 21, 75, 122
Dyer, Ralph L., 139

Ericson, August William, 45, 81
Escarda, Lenny, 96
Evans, David, 74, 75

Fischer, Margarita, 130-131
Foley, D., 90
Fountain, Susie Baker, xii, 73
Freese, C., 95
Fuller, Theodore, 90

Genzoli, Andrew M., 79
Gibson, Fred H., 90
Gibson, George, 90
Gordon, David E., 12, 22
Greggs, W., 95
Gregor, Otto C., 108
Gustafson, Carl, 140

Hall, Mr., 108
Hall, Miss Clara, 90
Hanna, Miss Clara, 108
Harte, Bret, 110
Huntington, Lucy A., 90, 95

Inman, F., 90
Irvine, Leigh Hadley, 74

Janssen, J. E., 90
Jones, Marie Croghan (Conry), 129

Kelley, Harry, 90
Kendall, David, xvi
Kinsey, Louis T., 90, 94, 105

Kyne, Peter Bernard, 20

Lee, Roland, 79
Lent, James B., 90
Libbey, H. A., 90

McCarthy, J., 95
MacDonald, S. A., 95
McFarland, Miss W., 95
McVicar, Allan A., 133

Madsen, Robert, 42, 43, 143
Monroe, Alonzo Judson, 105-108, 120, 131
Moore, Guy A., 4
Murray, George D., 96
Murray, John Gallagher, 90, 95

Palais, Hyman, xv-xvi, 13, 14
Palmquist, Peter E., xiii, 44, 80-81
Parker, J. Carlyle, 19
Persons, Louis, 95
Pickard, Dan, 73
Puter, L. F., 108

Rellinger, Miss M., 95
Richardson, H. S., 108
Richardson, Miss Lulu, 108
Roberts, Earl, 14
Roscoe, Mrs. Stanley, 96, 132
Russell, A. J. (Gus), 141-142

Schimps, Erich, xii
Schwartzkopf, Chet, 140
Shurtleff, Rev. T., 23
Simas, Frank, 133
Simpson, James, xvi
Skinner, B., 95
Soule, Charles Parsons, 89, 138
Speegle, Will N., 18, 140
Sweasey, Richard, 75

Taylor, Harry, 95
Taylor, W. W., 95
Thurston, Jack, 108
Turner, Leslie, 4

Vance, John, xvi, 74
Vemeer, Al, 4

Wells, Willard, 105, 125, 127, 128, 130
Whitney, E. L., 21
Wilson, Annie M., 75

INDEX

Young, Mrs. R., 108

Zane, Annie (Mrs. George D. Murray), 95, 96

ECONOMIC ROSTER

Arcata and Mad River Railroad, 128

Bank of Eureka, 18, 140

Bay Mill, 14, 73, 76

Bendixsen, H. D., shipbuilding, 16, 123

Bucksport and Elk River Railroad, 15

Buhne Hardware Company, 131

California Electric Company, 77

Carson Block, 87-89, 98, 105, 132-133

Crocker Brothers, 88

Dolbeer and Carson Lumber Company, 13, 14, 15, 16, 17, 18, 19, 20, 21, 23-24, 26, 73, 75, 78, 79, 123, 124, 141

Eel River and Eureka Railroad, xvi, 15

Eureka Chamber of Commerce, 3, 6, 15, 18, 74, 123

Eureka Redwood Company, 3

Gemmill and Gibbard, Cabinet Makers, 78

Humboldt Bay Mutual Relief Association, 19

Humboldt Bay Woollen Mills, 18

Humboldt County Bank, 18

Humboldt Federal Savings and Loan Association, 3

Humboldt Lumber Manufacturers' Association, 16

Humboldt Northern Railroad, 15

Humboldt Shoe Factory, 18

Janssen and Company, 88

Mathews, J. E., News Agency, 94

Milford Land Company, 15

Muley Mill, 13

Myrtle Grove Cemetery, 22

Northern Mountain Power Company, 18

Pink Lady, 42-43, 143

Pioneer Mill, 12

Randall, A. W., Banking Company, 88

Ryan and Duff, 13

Savings Bank of Eureka, 18

Shipping Memorabilia
 Brazilian, 12; *Champion*, 21; *City of Chester*, 75, 94; *Golden City*, 20; *Lottie Carson*, 16; *Quoddy Bell*, 13; *Ranger*, 16; *Relief*, 16; *Schooner Fleet* Roster, 16; *Tigris*, 13; *Wawona*, 16-17; *William Carson*, 16, 145

Sunset Memorial Park, 22

Weck, A. F., Drugstore, 78-79

Wells and Son's Drug Store, 105

Wunderlich Brothers, Photographers, 100, 105

CULTURAL ADJUNCTS

Architectural Exhibitions (U.C.S.B., 1968 and 1979), 32, 34

Architectural Styles (Gothic Revival)
 French Accent (Second French Empire), 29, 31, 36, 45
 Italianate, 29, 30, 36, 45, 73
 Stick-Eastlake, 29, 30, 31, 32, 33, 34, 39, 41, 45, 60, 75-76
 Queen Anne, 5, 29, 30, 31, 32, 33, 34, 41, 42, 45, 48, 62

Baird's Opera House, 94, 95

California Historical Society, xiii, 5, 11, 12

California Midwinter International Exposition (1894), 36-37, 41

Carson Park, 24

Christ Episcopal Church, 19, 22, 24, 132

Clarke Museum, 140

Comrades Amateur Company, 106

Eureka-Humboldt Public Library, 124

Historic American Buildings Survey, 11, 45, 146

Humboldt Club, 137-139

INDEX

Humboldt County Historical Society, 96, 131, 140, 143
Humboldt Dramatic Club, 90
Humboldt State University, xii, 80, 81, 95, 96, 100, 105, 138, 142, 143-144
Humboldt Wheelmen, 137
Ingomar Club, xiii, xvi, 3, 6, 56, 133, 139-143, 144-146
Ingomar the Barbarian, xii, 93, 94-96, 105, 111, 113-120, 126-127, 143-144
Ingomar Theatre
    construction, xiii, 78, 96-100, 105, 106, 129-130
    theatricals, 105, 125-128, 128-131
    Final Curtain Call, 131-132
Local Dramatic Club Plays
    Octoroon, 89-91
    Ingomar the Barbarian, 94-96
    Golden Giant, 105, 108-110
Masonic Lodge, xv, 43
Movie Productions
    Ruggles of Red Gap, 3
    Valley of the Giants, 3, 20
Non-Roster Personages
    Charles Crocker, 28; Michael Harry de Young, 36; Mark Hopkins, 28, 76-77; Collis Porter Huntington, 28; Harold Melvin Hyman, xi; Samuel Eliot Morison, xi-xii; Earl Pomeroy, x-xi; Louis Portal, 44; Leland Stanford, 28
Pratt's Opera House, 94
Russ Hall, 89, 91, 94
St. Louis Fair (1904), 37-38, 41-42
Theatre Margarita, 130-131
Travelling Stock Companies
    Colonial Stock Company, 130
    Gage and Keene Company, 96
    Rose Stillman Company, 125-126
    L. R. Stockwell Company, 105
    Janet Waldorf Company, 126-128
William Carson Memorial Community Center, 24

NATIONAL ROSTER

ARCHITECTURAL PERSONAGES

Andrews, Wayne, 48
Baird, Joseph Armstrong, Jr., 11, 12, 28, 33, 39, 45, 54, 58, 60, 62, 140
Bancroft, Ashley, xvi
Bangs, Edward Geoffrey, 5, 44, 53, 55
Davidson, Marshall B., 5, 48
Downing, Andrew Jackson, 39
Folsom, Merrill, 57
Gebhard, David, 5, 32, 33, 34, 35, 39, 41, 42, 74
Greenaway, Kate, 37
Henderson, John D., 32
Karp, Ben, 46-47
Kirker, Harold, 5, 27, 31, 55
Lewis, Oscar, 44
Lynes, Russell, 33
Maass, John, 2, 5, 12, 27, 29
Mulloy, Elizabeth D., 48
Nelson, S. D., 34
Newsom, Archie, 35
Newsom, John J., 34-35
Newsom, Joseph Cather, 34-42, 53-55, 58, 75-76
Newsom, Noble, 35
Newsom, Samuel, 34-42, 53-55, 58, 75-76, 87
Newsom, Samuel, Jr., 34
Newsom, Sidney, 35
Newsom, Thomas D., 34
Olney, Mr., 36
Perusse, Lyle F., 29, 47-48
Pierson, William H., Jr., 74
Richey, Elinor, 31, 80
Rogers, Meyric, 62
Smith, G. E. Kidder, 5
Vail, Wesley D., 29-30, 38
Von Breton, Harriette, 32
Wrenn, Tony P., 48

INDEX

THEATRICAL PERSONAGES

Anderson, James, 112
Anderson, Mary, 112, 113
Anthon, Charles, 111

Barry, Eleanor, 105
Boucicault, Dion, 89

Chesley, Gene, 133
Conway, Fred M., 112
Crisp, Donald, 130
Cruze, James, 3

Davenport, Jean, 112, 113, 117
Dean, Julia, 112, 113
Downing, Robert, 112
Dresser, Louise, 3

Eddy, Edward, 112

Foley, Hattie, 126
Fremont, A. W., 126

Gale, Minnie K., 112
Gordon, Mackenzie, 129
Greene, Clay, 109-110

Halm, Friedrich, 111
Harvey, Paul, 130
Horton, Edward, 3

Lovell, Maria, 111

McCullough, John Edward, 112, 113, 142

McGregor, Norval, 127
McMinn, George Rupert, 117-118
McVey, Mr., 127

Marlowe, Julia (Taber), 111, 112, 113
Mowat, Anna Cora, 112

Ogle, Charles, 3
O'Neill, Nance, 113

Parker, Mrs. Edward (née Amelia Sylvia), 112
Perry, Harry A., 112
Plympton, Eben, 112
Ponisi, Mme., 112
Provost, Mary, 112, 113

Rambeau, Marjorie, 130
Rankin, McKee, 110
Reid, Wallace, 3

Salvini, Tomasso, 112, 113
Schumann-Heink, Mme., 129
Stark, Mrs. James (née Sarah Kirby), 113, 117
Stillman, Rose, 125-126

Thumb, Mrs. General Tom, 129

Vandenhoff, Miss, 112
Vizard, Harold, 126

Waldorf, Janet, 126-127
Winter, William, 116-117